THE
FRENCH GARDEN
1500-1800

**World
Landscape
Art &
Architecture
Series**

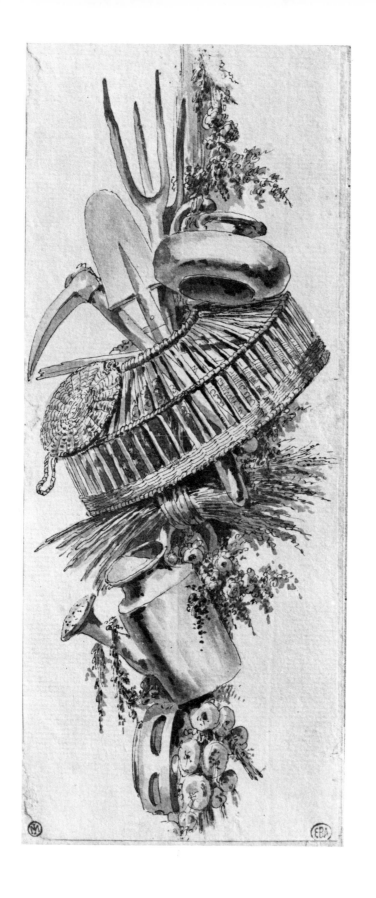

THE
FRENCH
GARDEN
1500-1800

WILLIAM HOWARD
ADAMS

GEORGE BRAZILLER
NEW YORK

For information address the publisher:

George Braziller, Inc.
One Park Avenue
New York, N.Y. 10016

Library of Congress Cataloging in Publication Data

Adams, William Howard.
  The French Garden, 1500–1800.

  (World landscape art and architecture series)
  Bibliography
  Includes index.
  1. Gardens, French—History. I. Title. II. Series.
SB457.65.A32   712′.0944   78–24655
ISBN 0–8076–0918–8
ISBN 0–8076–0919–6 pbk.

Front cover subject: *Bassin d'Apollon* by P.D. Martin in the
Musée de Versailles. Cliches Musées Nationaux, Paris.
Back cover subject: *Marly. La Fontaine de la Nymphe,* 1713. *Archives Nationales,
Paris. Frontispiece subject: Cartouche,* Delafosse. *Bibliothèque École des Beaux-
Arts, Paris.* Photo Giraudon.

Book design by RANDALL DE LEEUW

Printed in U.S.A.

Contents

Preface

The French garden is one of the celebrated and distinguishing elements of that civilization, as is its cuisine and code of manners. Rooted in an ancient tradition, subtly drawing upon and transforming inspirations from many sources, French landscape art represents a major contribution to Western culture. In its formal manifestation, before the landscape revolution of the eighteenth century, it was one of the most powerful images and symbols of the seventeenth century's Golden Age. Indeed, the influence of the French garden in theory and in practice was to dominate the rest of Europe with the stamp of French cultural and aesthetic ideals in a way that political ambitions, and the armies of Louis XIV, were never able to impose.

The aim of this book is to trace the development of the art and architecture of the French garden over the course of three hundred years by examining a number of the key examples in some detail. Not all of the great gardens could be mentioned, much less discussed. The extent and ramifications of French influence upon the gardens of the world beyond its borders had to be ignored. Nor is this book intended to provide a survey of purely "gardening" aspects, such as the use of plant materials, horticultural history, or the function of the garden as a utilitarian enterprise. All of these facets are, nevertheless, a part of French garden history, but will have to be developed from other sources.

The materials of garden history and garden art are among the most fugitive and ephemeral. Even the great monuments such as Versailles and Vaux-le-Vicomte are only outlines and shadows of their former grandeur. So much of the rich detail of plants and flowers, the pervasive sound of fountains and caged birds, above all, the important elements of music and declaimed poetry, are missing. These other sensual elements, beside the visual perfections, were essential to the French garden experience, and their absence can only leave those vast spaces bereft and sad. As Lionel Trilling once wrote, "Part of the melancholy of the past comes from our knowledge that the huge, unrecorded hum of implication was once there and left no trace." And nowhere is the absence of the activity that once animated the French garden felt more than on a cheerless day at Versailles, or walking in the park at Marly with one's imagination as sole companion.

Given the organic material of the garden, where nature itself works its endless changes on the face of the landscape through its cycles of growth and decay, it is difficult to be precise even about basic details of form, texture, and color in any given year or decade. Furthermore, in the great French gardens nothing was ever completely static. Both major and minor conceptual changes were constantly being introduced and tested, only to be replaced by more innovations and alterations. This quality, which is often forgotten, has made the subject even more complex from a historical point of view. For the student, documents in the form of plans and views and descriptions are critical. A first-hand knowledge of the topography is also essential.

In selecting the gardens singled out to construct the framework of this study, I have been guided not only by a close examination of the documents and manuscripts available, but by actually exploring and contemplating all of the surviving sites discussed. Some exist, as at Montceaux and Saint-Germain-en-Laye, as archaeological fragments. Others survive only in a vague topographical outline which can be traced on contemporary plans, as at Amboise and Gaillon. The celebrated gardens of Versailles, Vaux, and Chantilly, which were extensively restored in the nineteenth and twentieth centuries, can still convey something of their original quality and spirit, although they can be easily misinterpreted by the distorted photographic image that frequently is used to represent a quite different historic aspect. Because photographers have so often been tempted by the dramatic visual possibilities, at the expense of historic accuracy, few photographs have been included.

My work has been built on the foundation of many scholars, whose contributions are listed in the notes and bibliography. I have reinforced my own understanding not only through my field studies of the sites themselves, but also by attempting to master the basic plans and views which have been reproduced. My modest goal for the text is that it will encourage readers to regard more closely the visual documents provided, in order that they might draw their own conclusions, and to enable those who have an opportunity to explore first-hand the *grandes lignes* as well as the details of any one of the gardens discussed, to do so with a greater awareness of the history and complexities that lurk beyond a glance from the main terrace down the central avenue. That, after all, is only the beginning. The depth of a country's civilization, as Edith Wharton wrote, can, "to a great extent be measured by the care she gives to . . . the corner of her life where the supposedly useless arts and graces flourish." In the cultivation of the garden over the centuries "France has surpassed all modern nations; and one of the greatest . . . opportunities is to find out why."

The study of French garden history has lain dormant for several decades after a burst of activity, particularly among French scholars, earlier in this century. Even now the surface of the history of the heroic period of the French garden in the seventeenth century has hardly been scratched. No adequate study of the most consummate and best preserved example of the Grande Siècle, that of Vaux-le-Vicomte, now exists. Little in the way of a basic investigation of the sources of Le Nôtre's other great creations has been carried out. Nor, for that matter, is there an adequate biography of Le Nôtre, either in French or in English. Architecture, so long recognized as a fundamental influence upon the development of the garden in France, extending from du Cerceau to François Belanger, has rarely been considered from the point of view of its landscape setting, leaving a large area of conjecture and speculation regarding the respective roles of the architect and the landscape gardener or designer. When one speaks of de l'Orme or Boyceau, or even Le Nôtre, and their specific contribution to a garden layout, one must be very careful, since actual documentation is seldom available. When the reader encounters an attribution in the text, I urge him to allow some space for other names as well, to add to those principal figures the armies of artisans and craftsmen who also helped shape the extraordinary landscape creations we associate today with only one or two convenient labels.

Most recently, the field of French garden studies and related subjects, which can range from the *feu d'artifice* to urban history, has been opened up. Many of the scholars who have made important contributions participated in the Dumbarton Oaks Colloquium on the French Formal Garden held in 1974. In addition, Hamilton Hazelhurst's study of the great garden theorist Jacques Boyceau has been a substantial contribution. I should also mention Naomi Miller's eminently distinguished work on the French Renaissance fountain and the rich presentation of material in the exhibition organized by the *Caisse Nationale des Monuments Historiques et des Sites* on the garden revolution of the late eighteenth century. The exhibition has been documented in the illustrated catalogue produced by the staff of the Hôtel de Sully. Dora Wiebenson's study of the picturesque garden in France further extends and provides continuity to the material in the exhibition.

My debts are many. With no particular hierarchy, I should like to begin with the staff of the library of the National Gallery of Art and that of Dumbarton Oaks Garden Library headed by Elisabeth MacDougall, who provided an American base of operation for my investigations. This led to the work in French archives and libraries and to a number of field trips guided and assisted by an able and enthusiastic colleague, Patrick Bracco.

In France I have been generously allowed to help myself to the collections of the Cabinet des Estampes of the Bibliothèque Nationale, the Cabinet des Dessins of the Musée du Louvre, the Musée Carnavalet (and especially by M. Bernard de Montgolfier), the Musée de l'Île de France à Sceaux, the Archives Nationales, the Bibliothèque de l'Arsenal, the Musée Condé at Chantilly, and the Bibliothéque de l'Institute de France. At Versailles, Pierre Limoine opened all necessary doors and gates for whatever I needed. I am particularly grateful to Patrice de Vogüe at Vaux-le-Vicomte for his hospitality, and to Olivier Choppin de Janvry for his excellent introduction to the Désert de Retz, which he has defended, and helped to restore. Jean Cailleux was most generous in sharing the correspondence of Hubert Robert relating to his work at Méréville. Claude Malecot very kindly put at my disposal the photographs assembled for the exhibition *Jardins en France 1760–1820*. Alain Pougetoux at the Archives Photographiques of the Ministere de la Culture et de l'Environment made available many of the evocative garden photographs of Eugéne Atget for my pleasure. Naomi Miller has been a valued friend and critic along the way.

The months in London on two sabbaticals from the National Gallery were productive because of the superb help provided by the London Library. The resources of the British Library, The Library of the Victoria and Albert Museum, and the Courtauld Institute also supplemented my research in France.

To all the members of my family who have warmly supported me in my work I dedicate the results.

William Howard Adams
Hazelfield
1978

I. Learning From Paradise

The prodigious vision of the natural landscape transformed into a work of art has never been surpassed outside of France. A hundred years before Le Nôtre cast his new schemes onto the modest gardens of the old hunting lodge at Versailles, Jacques Androuet du Cerceau captured in his views and plans with their precise elegance, the majestic sweep of the earlier châteaux, parks, and gardens of the Valois civilization which then vanished. As dream-worlds of perfection, holding in balance a field of forces, of art and nature shaped into a green oasis of order, even the earliest French Renaissance gardens displayed an intricate, sophisticated system of ancient skills and traditions wielded into a coherent art form. Succeeding generations of some of France's greatest artists commanded and inspired by kings, princes, cardinals, and often their mistresses, would build on those foundations, piling up the dazzling results to astonish the world with garden splendor.

Du Cerceau's engravings which appear in various editions of *Les Plus Excellents Bastiments de France* are our best sources as we begin to trace the earliest outlines of this most transitory art, since nothing has actually survived. The new gardens recorded by du Cerceau in 1576–1579 and laid out during the opening decades of the sixteenth century coincided with the early stages in the evolution of France into a modern state. It was also a time, as we shall see, when the artistic life of France was beginning to display the borrowed finery of Italian culture worn over medieval habits, as Italian taste in the decorative arts, dress, manners, and gardens made itself felt throughout the country, following the military campaigns of Charles VIII, Louis XII, and Francis I between the years 1494–1525.

The first invasion of Italy by Charles VIII was mainly intended to settle dynastic claims with the kingdom of Naples but succeeded in introducing a generation of Frenchmen susceptible not only to the new humanist movement of classical learning that had spread from Florence to Milan, Naples, and other Italian cities, but to advanced principles of garden art unknown in France. Petrarch, whose works were studied in Paris before the Italian campaign, had understood the link between humanist learning and the garden in his own study of ancient literature and had carried his passion for both wherever he went, building gardens from Vaucluse to Tuscany. In a letter written in 1336 he described his latest garden creation as "shady, formed for contemplation and sacred to Apollo. It overhangs the source of the river, and is terminated by rocks and by places accessible only to birds."[1] Nearer his house, he continued, he had built a second "paradise" in the middle of a river and dedicated it to Bacchus. A grotto that he was confident resembled "the place Cicero sometimes went to declaim" was used for a study retreat.

For the adventurous young King Charles VIII, the road to Paradise was a tortuous trail leading south over the Alps and guarded by Italian strongholds that were captured one by one as in an ancient initiation rite. Finally, the Aragonese capital itself, recently rejuvenated under the leadership of Alfonso II, fell to the French invaders in February 1494, after the hysterical Alfonso had abdicated and fled to Sicily, carrying with him, it was said, seeds from his beloved Neapolitan gardens to start new ones in exile.

Even though his triumph was short-lived, lasting only five months, the King was deeply impressed by the luxurious palaces, gardens, and villas of Naples that Alfonso had built during his renewal programs. The gardens, with their elaborate hydraulic systems, fountains, and sculpture, were "an Earthly Paradise," Charles wrote to his brother-in-law, Pierre de Bourbon, after he had inspected his adversary's elegant villas of La Duchesca and Poggio reale.

The oriental luxury of La Duchesca and its astonishing gardens with spacious avenues, baths, marble fountains, and a hippodrome could only have reminded the King of the inadequacy of his own small, constricted garden courts within the fortress-château of Amboise. To Charles, the very idea that artists and craftsmen could create such a fanciful version of Paradise here and now on this earth was, in itself, something new. It was an energizing concept of the Italian Renaissance that was soon to spread throughout Europe and especially to France with the return of the soldiers and statesmen who had seen the New Eden.

Even when it became necessary to suddenly abandon Naples in July of 1495, the retreating French army carried with it enormous quantities of Italian art—"countless marvels" in the words of one chronicler—including tapestries, paintings, and sculpture to decorate the châteaux and abbeys of the now dissatisfied French upon their return home. From the standpoint of French garden history, the "reverse" invasion of the band of Italian garden craftsmen—such as Pacello de Mercogliano, a Neapolitan priest and *jardinier*, Fra Giocondo, Jerome Pacherot, Guido Mazzoni, and Domenico da Cortona—was to have a major impact on landscape art through the introduction of their ideas and methods. It is the result of the influence of these Italian craftsmen who worked at Amboise, Blois, Gaillon, and other châteaux of the Loire Valley and around Paris (though merged with the older French garden styles) that one sees in du Cerceau's illustrations. French gardeners quickly began to learn from the Italian visitors and to superficially apply the new concepts, at least initially, to the existing garden structures—though it would be difficult to disentangle the contributions of specific craftsmen or to distinguish the work as being either Italian or French.

While it inspired no direct imitation, Alfonso's new palace, Poggio reale, designed by the Florentine architect Guilano da Mariano, particularly impressed the French invaders. The reason why it captivated the French imagination can be easily understood. As a villa and garden designed for the sake of pure luxury and splendor, to serve as a theater and for other court entertainments, nothing like it had been seen along the Loire.

The pleasure palace was built around an arcaded courtyard with a recessed center surrounded by four tiers of seats forming an amphitheater which could be flooded for water spectacles. One side of the courtyard opened onto a garden, and through a park vista beyond, a dramatic view of Vesuvius was framed. Ornamental fish ponds, canals, and a central fountain with a terra-cotta sculpture group were sheltered by a garden pavilion, very much like those which would appear later in France.

French travelers, of course, had also seen and been impressed by other Italian gardens such as those of the Medici around Florence where the very essence of the humanistic Renaissance imagination was summed up in the open villas looking out over the countryside from their high terraces and "bounded by familiar mountains," in the words of Leon Battista Alberti. But the very theatrical quality and extravagance of Poggio reale separates it from most contemporary Italian

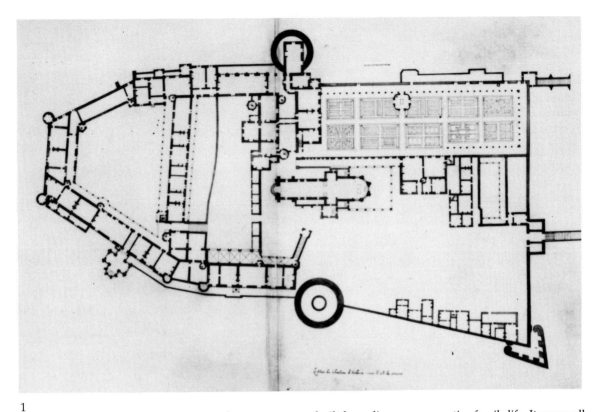

1

retreats and country manors built for ordinary, conservative family life. It may well have been this theatrical, nostalgic air of a villa ideal recalling ancient beauty and pleasures that had so captivated Charles, prompting him to compare it with Paradise.

Upon his entry into Naples, Charles had been greeted, rather disloyally, by the great humanist Giovanni Gioviano Pontano who had been one of Alfonso's teachers. In his *De splendore* Pontano had written a description of the ideal garden life of a Renaissance prince, evoking the pleasures that a retreat such as Poggio reale could provide as a place "for walking, or for banquets as the occasion demands. The gardens will have exotic plants and excellent little trees, very artificially and properly arranged." The function of gardens is different for the prince than for the ordinary man, Pontano continued, for not only do "gardens contribute wonderfully to the splendor of the villa," but they allow the prince "to shine not only in the city but in the country, least when he abandons the cares of the former he should seem to pass from light into shadow."[2]

Pontano's idea that the gardens of the princes and nobles must necessarily be distinguished had already been expressed by Petrus Crescentius of Bologna in his influential agriculture treatise first made public by the Angevin king of Naples in 1305 and later circulated in France. Quoting from classical writers, Petrus pointed out that while ordinary gardens were merely for production, the garden of the prince should be large, with grounds set aside for pleasure and all enclosed with a wall. Arbors, summer houses, and fish ponds should decorate the park through which a stream flows from a fountain and the woods should be filled with exotic birds and animals. A vista from the palace into the grounds would allow visitors to enjoy the wildlife from a distance.

Amboise and the other châteaux of the Loire at the beginning of the sixteenth century could not have been further from these early formulas for an Earthly Paradise, or from the splendid reality of Alfonso's Poggio reale. A solid, irregular medieval affair, Amboise had simply grown in response to military and domestic

2

3

pressures, and had little to recommend it beyond its spectacular setting above the river (Fig. 1). The garden plot that the Italian gardeners found within the fortress was a small, enclosed space near the burial ground, resembling the traditional layout of a medieval cloister one sees illustrated in contemporary Books of Hours or finds in the stereotyped literary descriptions of the period.

The gardens of the monasteries and abbeys in France, and elsewhere throughout the medieval world, had kept alive the useful gardening skills of plant cultivation, but the designing and planning of gardens to promote the splendor of the Church and the spread of the Faith was not a major function of the various religious orders. While the gardens of the cloister provided food and medicine for both body and soul, the traditional four-square layouts, sometimes following the lines of an ancient Roman foundation or ruin and planted with vegetables and herbs as well as flowers, were not without their formal, meditative appeal. The *potager* of the great châteaux in fact continued to be laid out in the formal, decorative style of the Middle Ages well into the seventeenth century. The peristyle of the Roman villa undoubtedly inspired the medieval cloister colonnade and the early Renaissance arcade, "a Paradise in Roman fashion" that would still later be translated into the *berceau* or green arbor (Fig. 2). Water for the garden and in a central location, either as a fountain or a well, was a practical necessity. Often the fountain was housed in a kiosk or small pavilion located at the intersection of the walks. This simple geometric organization defined the garden space which was focused on a central element, establishing a pattern at an early date that links these beginnings, as many historians have noted, to the classic *jardin de la raison* of the seventeenth century.

Whether or not a fountain within a trellised pavilion suitable for love and meditation as one sees in du Cerceau's engravings of Blois and Gaillon was actually built at Amboise is not certain (Fig. 3). The first time that the immigrant

Italian gardener Pacello's name appears in the accounts of Amboise, however, is in the role of hydraulic engineer to devise a way to bring water from the Loire up to the château, most probably for a fountain.

The elaborate use of water in the gardens of Poggio reale was essential to their composition, and enthralled Charles with its fountains, water tricks, and canals. It is clear that he intended his own terrestrial Eden to also be well supplied when he persuaded the plumber-humanist, Fra Giocondo, who had translated the classic text of Frontinus' *De Acquis urbis Romanae*, to come and work at the French court.

The lavish use of water was not unknown to medieval gardens of the thirteenth and fourteenth centuries. Nor, for that matter, were the other elements of early Italian Renaissance gardens complete innovations. The geometric format, symbolic division of spaces with poetic and religious associations, arbors and covered walks, Near Eastern plant material, menageries and aviaries were all familiar to the French garden vocabulary. Even the grotto, an example of which Charles probably saw in Naples and which was destined to become an important garden feature later in the sixteenth and seventeenth centuries, had been a part of Petrarch's garden at Fontaine de Vaucluse in the fourteenth century. The exotic garden that Robert d'Artois built at Hesdin on his return from the Crusades in 1270 displayed a strong oriental influence in its fountains, water tricks, automatons, and wild game park, recalling the Islamic "paradises" he had seen during his Eastern adventures.

The sudden death of Charles in 1498 did not halt the work he had only started at Amboise, for his successor, Louis XII, had also caught the building and landscape fever and continued to improve the royal châteaux and their gardens during the seventeen years of his reign. When he moved the court to Blois and rebuilt the castle on old foundations, he took with him both Pacello and Fra Giocondo. Even though the garden art of the early Italian Renaissance was imperfectly understood and interpreted during this transitional period, the gardens at Amboise and Blois were extended beyond the cramped spaces dictated by castle walls to challenge the immeasurable landscape outside the protected premises. This notion of an expanding space, freed also from the psychological restraints of the past and subject to new rules of organization, was a significant development and may be the chief legacy of these first Italian adventures (Fig. 4 and Fig. 5).

Had the Italian adventures by the French been a military success, who knows but that some future Gallic Hadrian in later centuries might have attempted to actually recreate physical features of a piece of his Italian empire in a corner of a French garden, much like the Emperor's famed villa at Tivoli. But, aside from a new sense of scale and a taste for Italian embellishments of sculpture and fountains, the French garden remained strikingly conservative. In spite of the possibilities of a new outward-reaching freedom suggested in the dramatic enlargement and extension of garden spaces beyond the confines of the old, fortified castle complex itself, most of the French gardens during the first half of the sixteenth century remained almost pathologically enclosed and static. Although the Florentines were building new country villas in picturesque settings with open courts and vistas beyond the garden itself into the countryside, the gardens at Amboise, Blois, and Gaillon, as one can see in du Cerceau's immaculate views, were still a series of walled, secluded spaces and not completely liberated either visually or spiritually.

At Blois and Gaillon, where the steep, irregular site dictated by earlier considerations of defense forced the gardens on to different levels, there was little attempt to create a harmonious relationship between the disparate parts, or even in relationship to the château itself. In its secretive, disjointed organization one is reminded of the early Renaissance descriptions of a garden found in Boccaccio, where the garden is totally separate from the house and, as Eugenio Battisti points out, even requires a special key to open its locked door.[3]

The arbored galleries one sees running along the sides of the garden at Blois,

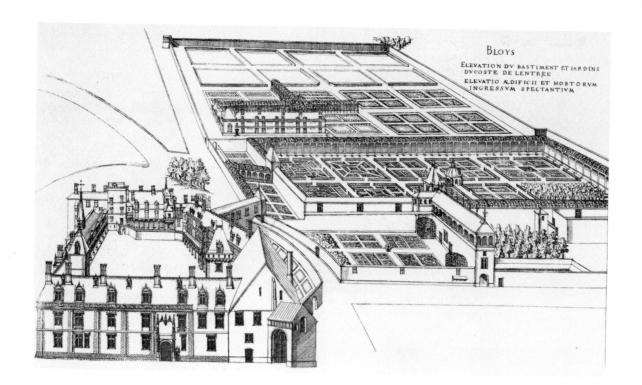

BLOYS

ELEVATION DV BASTIMENT ET IARDINS
DVCOSTE DE LENTREE
ELEVATIO ÆDIFICII ET HORTORVM
INGRESSVM SPECTANTIVM

4

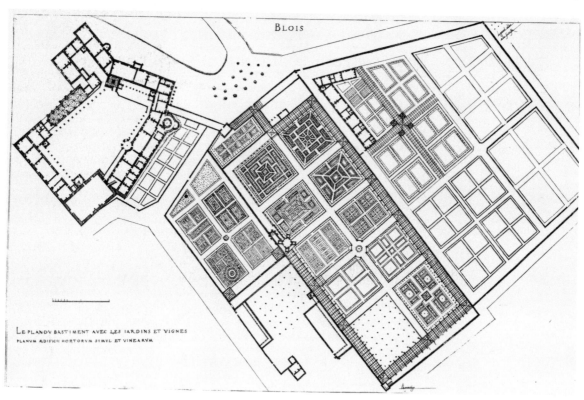

BLOIS

LE PLAN DV BASTIMENT AVEC LES IARDINS ET VIGNES
PLANVM ÆDIFICII HORTORVM SIMVL ET VINEARVM

5

14

with their elaborate medieval wood vaults on supporting columns, as has already been noted, suggest the cloister or perhaps the Roman peristyle, giving them an archaic quality.[4] But some scholars have hinted at an interpretation of these garden bowers as a Renaissance attempt to recreate the original, primeval shelter, recalling the theory of the origin of architecture advanced by Vitruvius: with men "working everything easily with their hands; they started to make roofs of branches."[5] Certainly, throughout the history of gardens from the Renaissance to the nineteenth century, decorative elements evoking a fantasy of the past and creating a mood of nostalgia in an attempt to recapture a lost world are a part of the garden's image.[6] As we shall see later in the Romantic period, the experiment to recreate Adam's house in Paradise within the framework of the landscape garden was to become even more explicit.

The finely patterned *parquets* (as the flower beds were called in the early accounts) that one sees in the drawings and engravings of du Cerceau, although dating from the middle of the sixteenth century, strongly suggest the geometric forms of flower beds in earlier medieval miniatures, paintings, and books, reinforcing the continuity of the traditional, conservative design of the early French Renaissance gardens (Fig. 6).[7] The illuminations found in *Rustican de Librus des Champs* by Petrus Crescentius (who became Pierre de Crescent when he was translated into French in 1516) show comparable geometric parterres planted with herbs and small trees.[8] Iron (or wood) railings enclose each of the raised beds, a fashion that could still be seen in Parisian gardens as late as the end of the eighteenth century.

The nostalgia for the past—both classical and Christian—is nowhere more clearly evoked than in Francesco Colonna's *Hypnerotomachia Poliphili* first published in Venice in 1499.[9] Its rich literary and visual backdrop to the lover's search for his beloved through a profusion of antique architectural fantasies and gardens appealed to the French imagination, perhaps because it resembled in many respects its medieval predecessor, the *Roman de la Rose*, as Naomi Miller has pointed out.[10] John Summerson calls Colonna's dreamy vision of the Golden Age "the romantic, haunted, introverted side" of the Renaissance which was grafted onto the more rational architectural theories advanced by Alberti, and also embraced by French students in their efforts to reconstruct a picture of the classical world, its buildings and its gardens.[11] In Colonna's epic, the pagan gods of the ancient world remain alive in the cultural setting and ritual of the late Middle Ages, and his naturalistic vocabulary is actually drawn from descriptions in Pliny the Elder's *Natural History*. Classical fantasies of architecture become the setting for Christian ritual in Colonna's gardens. The medieval "Fountain of Salvation" becomes the backdrop of a garden love scene and the nymphaeum of antiquity, a Platonic baptistry (Fig. 7).[12]

In the first French edition of *Hypnerotomachia*, called *Le Songe de Poliphile*, the illustrations are more elegantly drawn, and there is a greater emphasis on architectural detail than in the Italian original, enabling them to be used by artists and garden designers for the next hundred years, even appearing as a possible ancestor of Mansart's Colonnade in the garden of Versailles, built in 1680.

Water is a major element in Colonna's romance, and the decorative fountains which magically transform its visual and auditory qualities are illustrated, becoming a virtual catalogue of these important, symbolic instruments. "Bound to life and love, to purification and healing, the imagery of the fountain" — so well summed up in Professor Naomi Miller's words—"could now incorporate that of its erotic antique predecessors to create a dazzling set-piece that would supersede mere practical requirements."[13]

The techniques of conducting large quantities of water from one place to another over uneven terrain, for useful as well as aesthetic purposes, continually challenged the engineering skills of the early Renaissance. Raising water from rivers to high terraced gardens required great hydraulic ingenuity. Creating the

necessary pressure to send a stream shooting from a fountain to match the imaginative descriptions of a Colonna or other contemporary flights of poetic fancy recalling the antique gardens of a well-watered Golden Age was a measure of scientific progress. Efforts to solve these complex water problems run as a leitmotif throughout French graden history from Amboise, Blois, and Gaillon to the hydraulic disasters created by Louis XIV to satisfy the insatiable fountains and water displays of Versailles and Marly.

In the hills above the Seine some thirty miles southwest of Rouen, the mutilated shell of Gaillon stands as a ghostly souvenir of the most important architectural achievement of the period.[14] It was built by Georges d'Amboise (1460–1510), who was made Cardinal in 1498. An ambitious, cultivated man, with designs on the papacy, d'Amboise had spent a great deal of time in northern Italy on military and state missions, and had met Leonardo da Vinci and other Italian artists and intellectuals.

Like the castles of Amboise and Blois, Gaillon, begun in 1502, was not a completely new creation, for an earlier foundation and some existing structures determined the plan of the fortress-palace. Its splendor was proverbial throughout France, the result of vast sums of money and the use of the best French and Italian talent available. Even Isabella d'Este Gonzaga received a detailed report on the castle, its contents and the gardens from the Mantuan envoy to the French court (Fig. 8).

The gardens of Gaillon which had been designed by Pacello de Mercogliano were again separated from the château itself as at Blois and Amboise.[15] One entered the main garden, which formed the middle terrace, by crossing a bridge from the central gate of the palace, then passing through an elaborate garden entrance to a wide walk that ran in a straight line through the middle of the space to the garden pavilion in the center and on to the two-storied casino built in the center of the far wall. On the upper terrace was a tree garden, and on the opposite side of the main parterre was another parallel terrace garden of elaborate, ornamented beds and orchard, which was, however, completely isolated by an imposing gallery that separated the two terraces. When one recalls that the Villa Madama—with its open loggia, communicating stairs, and integrated, symmetrical composition linking architecture and garden—is almost contemporary with

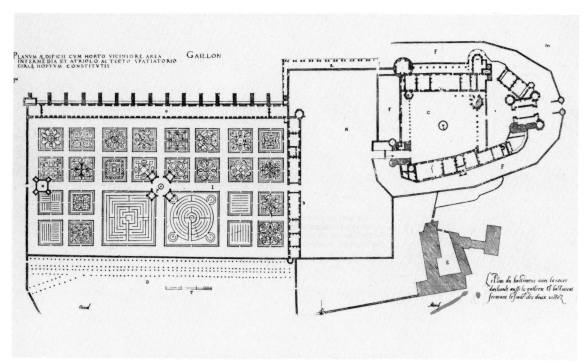

8

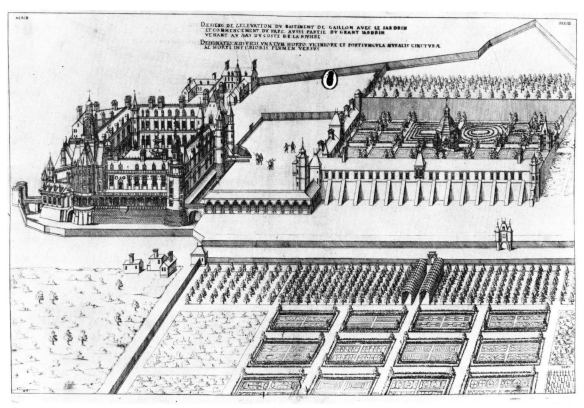

9

GAILLON

FONS MARMORÉVS
SITVS IN AREA

LA FONTAINE DE
MARBRE DANS LA COVRT

10

Gaillon, the actual distance in garden art between Italy and France becomes apparent. At Gaillon, the possibilities of the terraced site itself are ignored as also had been the case at Blois, and the use of ramps or stairs to achieve an architectural unity did not as yet seem a possibility. The garden experience was still enclosed, limited, and inward-looking, with something of the protective, cloistered spirit that enveloped the medieval *hortus* with its high walls, covered arbors, and four-square divisions (Fig. 9).

What was certainly a major achievement at Gaillon were the fountains, surpassing even their Italian counterparts of the period. In these most important Renaissance fountains, the very idea of all the later French garden fountains at Fontainebleau, Vaux, Petite-Bourg, Versailles, and Marly was prefigured. The fountain as a useful source of water was subordinated and transformed into a display, a symbolically ladened conceit, a royal work of art (Fig. 10). Cardinal d'Amboise, *"emulateur des vertus romains,"* combined all of those special qualities of the obsessed patron willing to spare nothing in order to organize and control the display of water, qualities so important in realizing the great garden spectacles in the next century.[16] The *"grande fontaine de marbre blanc, bien enrichie d'oeuvre,"* as described by du Cerceau, rose twenty-two feet in the air and was surmounted, appropriately, by a statue of John the Baptist.[17] It was placed in the "court of honor" but not quite on an axis with the smaller garden fountain that stood enclosed in its supremely elegant temple at the center of the great parterre. This latticed pavilion was similar to those at Amboise and Blois, though more elaborate, with aviaries built into its four corners so that the sound of the birds was combined with that of the splashing fountain to reinforce within its sheltering space the allegory of the Garden of Salvation, the Garden of Love, and the sensual pleasures of an Eastern paradise.

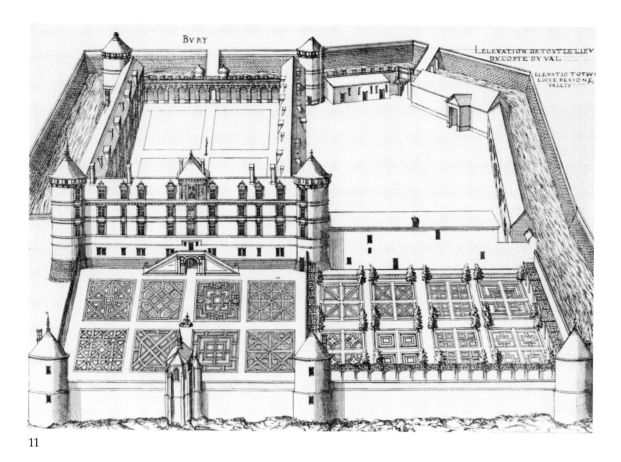

11

The main fountain in the *cour d'honneur* had been carved in Italy and had been shipped from Genoa to Honfleur in 1508. From there, and at enormous expense, it was taken along the Seine and then over a specially built road to the new château. Isabella Gonzaga must have been astonished and not a little envious to read her envoy's report describing the jet that rose seven feet in the air above the marble— "lactating Graces and micturating youths" — for such a splendidly mannered water piece had not yet appeared in Italy, not even for a Medici.

To single out the water displays in the gardens of Blois and Gaillon is not to suggest that they were unique in French gardens in the early part of the sixteenth century. Fountains are evident in a number of du Cerceau's plans, as for example at Bury, built by Florimond Robertet between 1511 and 1524, where a fountain can be seen in the center of the great parterre (Fig. 11). The strong axial symmetry and regularity of the plan suggest the hand of Fra Giocondo, though the evidence is not conclusive. In the center of the *cour d'honneur* at Bury, Robertet, who, like Charles VIII and Georges d'Amboise, had the imagination, opportunity, and means, displayed in his garden his appreciation of contemporary Italian art. There he placed a bronze version of Michelangelo's *David*, a gift he had received as a present from the Republic of Florence, surrounded by four large, flat, unornamented grass squares.[18] The austerity of the setting must have seemed sublime. Because of its height, it is likely that the statue could be glimpsed from the portico of the chapel by looking across the fountain in the middle of the parterre and through the doorways of the château itself.

Caption Notes *Chapter 1*

Fig. 1—This drawing of *Amboise* by Jacques Androuet du Cerceau was made after 1566 and was later engraved for *Les Plus Excellents Bastiments de France.* Plants recommended by early writers for making the figures of the compartments included basil, camomile, daisy, hyssop, marjoram, parsley, sage, sorrel, thyme. Borders were outlined in lavender, rosemary, myrtle. Box was used later. The disposition and inward planning of the enclosed garden space is medieval in its style and limitations. Its center is fixed and stable, reflecting a fixed and stable universe. (British Museum)

Fig. 2—Garden scene from Colonna's *Hypnerotomachia Poliphili* first published in 1499. The novel's Garden of Love was a source of inspiration for French gardens during the next two centuries. The fanciful designs in this illustration were derived from ancient prototpyes. (From *Edizione critica e commenti a cura di Giovanni Pozzi e Lucia A. Ciapponi, Padova, 1964,* Dumbarton Oaks Garden Library)

Fig. 3—View of the garden pavilion at *Amboise.* Although engraved by Israel Silvestre in the seventeenth century, the form of the building housing the fountain follows earlier designs. (Collection of the author)

Fig. 4—*Blois.* The first gardens at Blois were laid out in the fourteenth century. Du Cerceau's engraving from *Les Plus Excellents Bastiments de France* shows gardens extending far beyond the walls of the château by the middle of the sixteenth century. The upper space separated by an arbored wall was the *potager.* (Dumbarton Oaks Garden Library)

Fig. 5—*Blois.* The large central pleasure garden of ten squares separated by a central walk is an enlargement of the basic medieval four-square division. A fountain is at the center of the third cross-axis. The pavilion on the left appears to have four aviary cages at its corners similar to the pavilion at Gaillon. Separated physically from the château, the space has taken on an idealized quality remote from the everyday world of the castle. (Dumbarton Oaks Garden Library)

Fig. 6—*Garden of Love.* Miniature from *Le Roman de la Rose,* fifteenth century. (British Museum)

Fig. 7—Colonna's views of the ideal Renaissance garden life of sensual pleasures widely influenced the role of the garden as a civilized habitation. (Dumbarton Oaks Garden Library)

Figs. 8 – 9 — *Gaillon.* Georges d'Amboise began the work on the new château and garden around 1501. Though separated by a wide courtyard, the central walk of the main garden with two labyrinth compartments on one side is related to the château's courtyard. The *potager* was on the lower level. (Cabinet des Estampes, Bibliothèque Nationale)

Fig. 10—The great fountain at Gaillon engraved by du Cerceau for *Les Plus Excellents Bastiments.* The figure of John the Baptist crowned the top of the 22-foot high, richly ornamented marble work. It was finally dismantled in 1757. (Dumbarton Oaks Garden Library)

Fig. 11—*Bury* was built by Louis XII's minister, Florimond Robertet, between 1511 and 1524. A marked step toward the integration of the garden with the architecture, incorporating a regular plan, gives Bury a special significance. Michelangelo's *David* can be seen in the middle of the green squares of the upper courtyard. The *potager* at the lower right communicates with the large farmyard above it.

II. Grottos, Water,
and Other Garden Fantasies

Even though it continued to function as a pleasure retreat, the elaborate framework of the sixteenth-century garden, with its growing luxury and profusion of symbolic devices, pseudoclassical settings, grottos, statuary, ornamental water, artificial mounts, and spectacular pageantry, was directed gradually toward aesthetic, intellectual, and political ends. Festivity and rich, sensual diversions set the grounds of Fontainebleau, Anet, and Meudon apart from normal dwellings. Nature succumbed to the whims of the exalted.

Against this exotic background created by a society bent on rediscovering and reinterpreting the antique world by means of architecture and gardens, it was inevitable that the motif of the grotto would emerge, first in Italy and later France. Poems, romances, and ancient literature made innumerable references to sacred caves as retreats and earthly paradises—the locus of sacred memory and contemplation where the waters themselves were rejuvenating and transforming. A mixture of an imitation of a Roman bath and of natural caverns, the Renaissance grotto appeared as a luxurious hybrid creation of villa, garden ornament, and ancient nymphaeum. For the Renaissance it was the perfect vehicle to express the ambiguity of both its love of nature and the cult of the artificial. Exotic materials—precious stones, mosaics, stucco work, mirrors, and coral—were used to enhance the fantasy of these strange places.

The first important Renaissance example of the architectural grotto was in the Palazzo del Tè at Mantua, designed by Guilio Romano and assisted by Francisco Primaticcio before he departed for France in 1532. Primaticcio's experience at the Gonzaga court undoubtedly influenced his work at Fontainebleau, where he worked with Serlio on the *Grotto des Pins* in 1543 (Fig. 12). The new grotto was actually built into a corner of a pavilion of the château as a kind of stone porch facing the *jardin des pins*, not far from the *cour du Cheval Blanc*. Its façade was formed by four sturdy Atlases cut in the rough stone who appear to hold in place the three heavily rusticated arches. As a haunt for nymphs, the stuccoed interior (in contrast to the rustic exterior) was ornamented with seashells and mosaic, while Juno and Minerva from the fresco on the ceiling presided over elaborate fountains that played into a central basin.[1] The grotto, like the garden as well as the palace, was rich with metaphor in its decoration.

In 1552 Primaticcio's great villa-palace for the Cardinal de Lorraine, the *Grotte de Meudon,* was begun on the dramatic terraced slope of the Cardinal's estate overlooking the Seine near Paris. Vasari in his *Life of Primaticcio* said that "one might well call it the Thermae on account of its resemblance to that type of ancient edifice and because of the size and quantity of the loggie, staircases and public and private apartments it contains" (Fig. 13).[2] Theatrically placed as the climax to the garden layout, the central pavilion, flanked by smaller wings at some distance, was centered on a fifteen-bay cryptoporticus that formed the substructure of the great terrace-stage. The two end pavilions were linked to the central structure by diagonal stairs and were tied to the garden itself by ceremonial steps leading down onto the terrace at either end of the arcaded base. The series of terraces and connecting stairs suggests a kinship with Bramante's Belvedere courtyard and the ancient Roman temple at Palestrina. The strong symmetrical lines of the terraces dominate and frame the garden, spread like a carpet below, to balance and echo the building itself, creating a unity between the garden and the architecture that is both festive and pastoral. The interior of Meudon sparkled with mosaics and enamelwork depicting an elaborate iconography. Flowing streams of water and jetting fountains enhanced the antique atmosphere. The sanctuary of these inner rooms was rather small in contrast to the monumental splendor of the façade, heightening the mannerist contrast and confusion between the clear, architectonic exterior and the mysterious, dark artifice of the secret world inside (Fig. 14).

In an ode celebrating the royal wedding at Meudon in 1559 of Claude de France, the daughter of Henri II to Charles, the Duc de Lorraine, the poet Pierre Ronsard, who participated in the ritual disguised as a shepherd, captured the ceremonial and mystical atmosphere of the place in his nostalgic imagery evoking an antique arcadia, as he approached the grotto.

> While their cattle cropped the grass plain, slowly they ascended to the grotto of Meudon, where young Charles, whose name is sacred to the woods, had built a retreat lovely enough to be the eternal dwelling of the Nine Sisters. Then they took courage and entered the hallowed, fearful cavern where, as if touched by divine fire, they felt their minds suddenly gripped by an insensate passion. They stood amazed to see so fine a building erected in such a lonely waste, with stately plan and façade and rustic pillars rivaling the grandeur of antique columns; to see how on the walls Nature had portrayed the liveliest grotesques in flinty rock; to see halls, apartments, chambers, terraces, festoons, checkered and oval designs and enamel bright with many colors. . .[3]

In order to bring enough water from the river below up to the fountains of Meudon's "lonely waste," the Cardinal, who greatly admired the ornamental use of water at Tivoli, hired Philibert de l'Orme to engineer an elaborate conduit and pumping system. It was not a success, and de l'Orme's failure to deliver the water to the grotto prompted Bernard Palissy to recommend that gardens be placed at the foot of hills so that the water could flow down from the springs and reservoirs by gravity. Water was more important than the view.

Palissy, that eccentric, persecuted potter, naturalist, and garden designer, managed to combine both practical gardening experience with poetic imagination, if one can judge from his writings since, unfortunately, none of his garden works have survived. His *Recepte Véritable,* first published in 1563, describes an ideal garden "so lovely that it is second to none in the whole world except the earthly paradise." The garden was of the most startling design and included four grottos carefully camouflaged beneath rocks and shrubs. In 1563, Palissy, known as *"inventeur des rustiques figurines du roi,"* also published an entire book on the subject of grottos entitled *Architecture et Ordinance de la Grotte Rustique.* The grottos he described were in fact modeled on the magnificent underground invention he had started for Anne de Montmorency at Ecouen, as a kind of retreat from the religious wars, and later actually built in Catherine de'Medici's garden at the Tuileries.

Inside Palissy's grotto, which he claimed was true to nature, the walls were covered with faïence lizards, snakes, birds, and vegetables made by the potter. At one end, water fell from a terrace of simulated rocks made of terra-cotta into a pool lined with glistening fish also made of faïence. In fact, it was part of Palissy's

12 L.D. 60

13

14

15

16

scheme to constantly confront the visitor within the cave with elements of "reality," which, on close inspection, turned out to be intricate deceptions of the potter's art. Colonna's *Hypnerotomachia* was one of Palissy's favorite books, and it undoubtedly inspired Palissy with incipient romantic descriptions of grottos where artificial reptiles made of faïence were embedded in the walls and pools.

One of the most astonishing structures in Palissy's ideal garden is a green temple built of living trees planted and trained into classical columns. Carefully administered cuts "cause the deposit of fresh wood and nature protuberances that shall correspond to the pedestals and capitals . . ."[4] A similar technique is recommended to form the pillars of the amphitheater. On the top of the theater is a kind of wind sock that gathers the wind in its mouth and carries it to a series of musical instruments that automatically respond. The theater itself is built on a small island and is enclosed with a wire net to form a splendid aviary so that the music of the wind, the singing birds, and the encircling water create a kind of natural symphony—a piece of garden invention that would have made even Hadrian envious. The display of birds in aviaries in French gardens has a long history and was as popular as fishponds, game preserves, and menageries. As a forerunner of the zoo, elaborate buildings were designed to house both wild animals and rare birds.

17

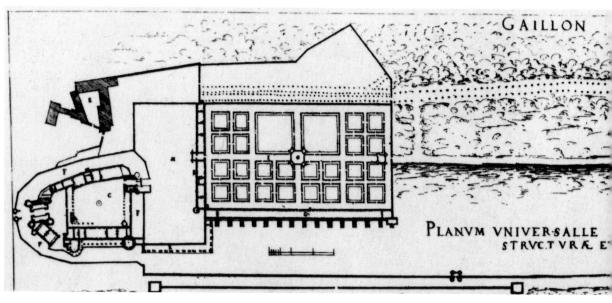

GAILLON

PLANVM VNIVERSALLE
STRVCTVRÆ E

At Versailles, the menagerie became so grand that it contained a suite of apartments and a salon in the middle where, according to Félibien, *"une grande Princesse va souvent gouter les plaisirs de la compagne et de la solitude."*

Marie de'Medici maintained an aviary in the garden of the Tuileries near the amphitheater where the public could enjoy the bird concert. It was an old custom to place cages of singing birds in the garden and then cover the cages with branches so that visitors could hear them and enjoy a temporary illusion of being in a wild forest. Birds and fountains were often combined, as in the pavilion at Gaillon and at Fontainebleau, where the volary was large enough to hold tall trees and two fountains. Birds were such an integral part of the garden that the earliest garden books like *La Maison Rustique* discussed critically the relative musical quality of various bird species.

Among the decorations for the gardens at Chenonceaux, also ordered by Palissy's patron Catherine de'Medici, were grottos and fountains combining art and natural elements into an imitative theme, anticipating by one hundred and fifty years André Le Nôtre's playful little garden of springs at Trianon. The main feature, the *Fontaine du Rocher,* was not unlike the nymph-festooned rock seen earlier wheeled into the ballet at the Tuileries during the fête Catherine staged for the Polish ambassadors. Streams of water poured from the artificial mount as if they were natural springs, and ran down the rough surface to the large basin below. A contemporary account of the gardens of the Tuileries written in 1575 mentions a similar fountain in the form of a rock where Palissy's faïence frogs, snails, and vipers appeared to crawl over the wet surface.

The use of an extravagant artificial rock as the source of a fountain, introducing the purifying and transforming quality of water and confusing illusion with reality, appealed to the predilections of that ambiguous age (Fig. 15). The ornamental rock or *rocher* representing Parnassus, the mountain of the muses, in festival sets and garden fountains was often combined with a grotto at its base, as can be seen in many engravings of court productions in the sixteenth and seventeenth centuries (Fig. 16). Together with its classical allusions there are also lurking suggestions of Christian symbolism.

At Gaillon, where Cardinal Charles de Bourbon, who had succeeded Georges d'Amboise, commissioned a garden complex of a *rocher,* canal, and nymphaeum in 1550, we see a superb example of what Eugenio Battisti has called "the Renaissance picturesque" (Fig. 17).[5] The *Maison Blanche,* a two-story marble pavilion, was placed on an island in the middle of an artificial lake that formed a canal running on its axis to a strange artificial mound or *rocher,* known as the "Parnassus de Gaillon." Du Cerceau, who engraved the plates of the complex, and referred to

Merid   PP

NIVM OMNIVM TOTIVS LOCI
ŒNIORVM FARTIVM

Occid

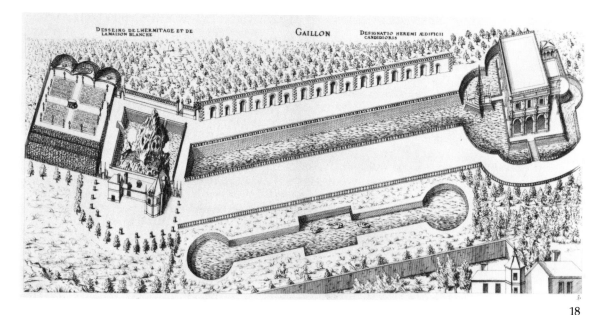

it as "a place of isolation full of pleasures," may well have been the architect, for the ensemble resonates with a picturesque, even romantic imagination (Fig. 18). Both the formal Italianate pavilion and the *rocher* contained a grotto — one "natural," the other completely architectural. Paralleling the main pool and linking the *Maison Blanche* with the enclosed mount is a separate canal, suggesting in its arbitrary relationship and symmetry, with the two circular pools at either end, the erotic water architecture of Persia.

Apparently the *Maison Blanche* was built as a permanent theater set for entertainments, a stage cleanly cut out of the hillside above the main park and placed on an artificial platform. In 1566 when the Cardinal entertained Catherine de'Medici, during the siege of Rouen, the *Maison Blanche* was used for a pastoral masque in the style of the elaborate festivities staged at Fontainebleau and Meudon. In the exotic, sensual, and extravagant decor, surrounded by water, the total animated experience, elevated by music and poetry, must have approached the baroque scenography of opera that was to emerge later in no less dramatic settings in the Italian courts. Imagining the sound of the trumpets tilted to the sky, the roll of the drums, and the flashes of richly costumed courtier-actors reflected in water mirrors helps to animate the French garden of the sixteenth century in one's imagination as nothing else could. Indeed, color, movement, and sound were essential elements of Renaissance garden life as it became more public and open.

Opposite the *Maison Blanche* the craggy, artificial mountain or "hermitage," reached by a drawbridge, almost fills the square pool surrounding it. On one side of this hallowed retreat is a small chapel suggesting a religious function, although its exact use remains a mystery. The miniature mountain, contained in a box like a sacred relic, evokes the jagged cliffs above Saint Jerome's hermitage painted by Joachin Patinir (now in the Prado). Within the formal setting of architecture and water, and as an eccentric, romantic refuge within the larger tableau, du Cerceau recreated a medieval vision of extraordinary power and tension, where both reality and art are inverted by mystery and obscurity.

Few elements in the plans of the gardens of the sixteenth century gardens are as pervasive as the presence of water. It dominates the earliest garden layouts at Chantilly, Fontainebleau, and Dampierre. The bold and superbly manipulated surfaces of still water are in sharp contrast with the architecture and surrounding landscape — the shimmering reflection of light playing against the sky and the vegetation, distorting perspectives and heightening the illusion of the garden as a dream. Eleanor Clark has suggested that water was used as a powerful narcotic to create the illusionary atmosphere of Hadrian's villa, thus subduing in its distortions the overbearing, imperial architecture. "Water," Clark writes, "was a prime element in architecture, here as in Rome, an element to be given shape, form, like other materials, subject to conception as varied—left flat and still or used in other simple ways on occasion, but more elaborate in its faces and kinds of motion. It is the element of distance and the undefinable co-medium of light, serving purposes of luxury, that later when indoors were really indoors and glass was better, were taken over by wall-length mirrors and crystal chandeliers."[6]

The water trenches or moats that first surrounded the medieval French château were, of course, designed for protection and defense against the disorders of the outside world. Symbolically, the water enclosure was also a way of creating an artificial island to protect man not only from military enemies, but also to separate him psychologically from wild nature itself with all the implications of the primitive fear of the natural world and chaos that had haunted Western man for centuries. The medieval fortresses of Fontainebleau and Chantilly, for example, had been placed in watery marshes that provided a natural protection. When the center of gravity of a unified monarchy in the sixteenth century spawned the building or rebuilding of châteaux and gardens in the Île de France on an unprecedented scale — throwing off the walled and moated medieval life which was particularly restrictive during the Hundred Years War — water was released for new ornamental purposes.

The castle of Chantilly itself was an island surrounded by a large body of water evoking one of man's oldest and most enduring romantic images, one that, from Homer to Robinson Crusoe, has held a powerful grip on the imagination (Fig. 19). Other castles encircled by water moats also suggested island realms that were in their isolation like the mermaid in the harbor of Copenhagen, "a thrilling defiance of nature," in the words of Charles Moore.[7] French architects understood the aesthetic and philosophical implications of the formal use of water in the

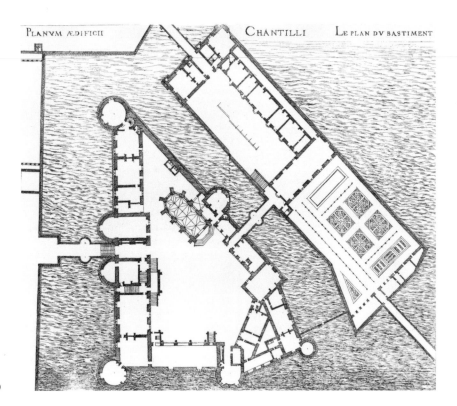

19

landscape. It was this long infatuation that informed the great water gardens of the seventeenth century. A sheet or *nappe* of still water as a mirror has an inviolable quality and became, as Christopher Tunnard has observed, "an instrument of fearful meaning."[8] The use of these water mirrors allowed French garden designers to assert their mastery over nature with the imposition of rational, precise outlines of calm reflections held firmly in place.

Probably the finest of the early canal-water gardens was that of the exquisite small château of Dampierre near Boissy on the Seine created by Cardinal de Lorraine beginning in 1550 when the old castle was pulled down (Fig. 20). The new château and its immediate enclosed garden space, built on regular lines, were placed within a formal rectangular water basin. At one end of the private garden where the walls formed a wide angle, a bathing pavilion or *thermae* was placed as a focus of the central walk and can be seen at this point. To the left of the château in du Cerceau's engraving of Dampierre is a moated garden composed of twenty-four intricately worked, square beds grouped into four large parterres. The garden appears to be surrounded with a low hedge providing an open view into the countryside and clearings beyond. Certainly the flat, unobstructed bodies of water and ornamental moats that one sees a Dampierre, Chantilly, and Fontainebleau encouraged the transformation of the inward looking, enclosed medieval garden, much as the sunken fence opened up the English garden in the eighteenth century.

At the Château de Vallery, extensively rebuilt around 1550 and called one of the *"plus belles et plaisantes maisons de la France,"* the abutting gardens with ornamental canals are separated by a raised terrace (Fig. 21).[9] A handsome galleried pavilion running across the terrace at mid-axis of the plan between the two gardens enabled the viewer to establish a coherent relationship with the surrounding landscape by looking over the lake below. The water from the upper garden passed through the lower canal basin in the center before it flowed into the ornamental lake (Fig. 22).

20

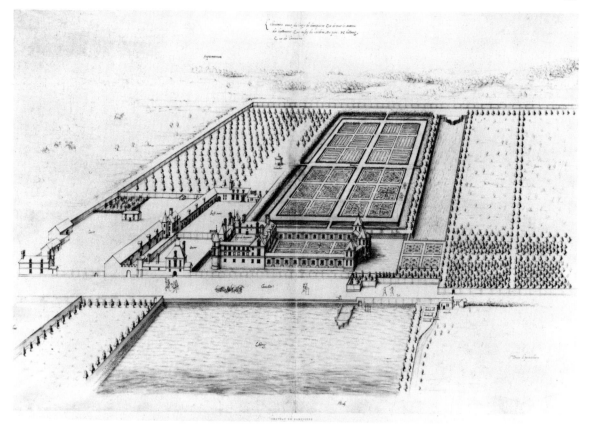

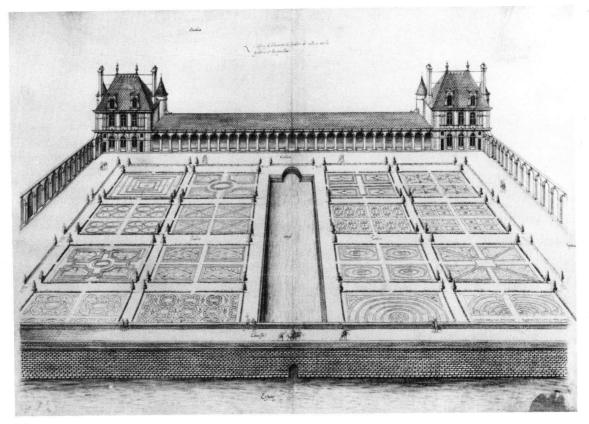

21

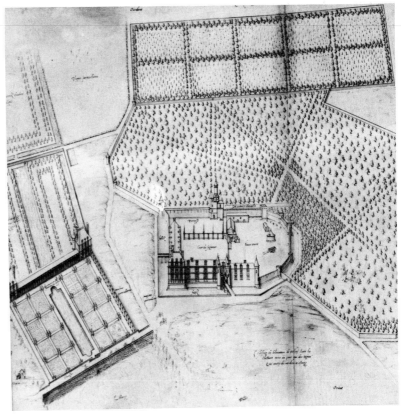

22

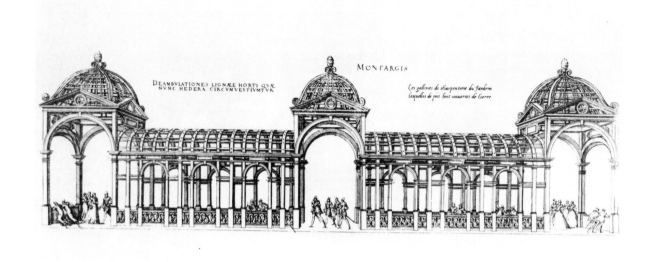

MONTARGIS

DEAMBVLATIONES LIGNÆE HORTI QVÆ.
NVNC HEDERA CIRCVMVESTIVNTVR

Ces gallories de charpenterie du Jardinn
lesquelles de pns sont couuertes de lierre

The *jardins de plaisir* of the first half of the sixteenth century, with their extensive use of terraces, reflected the growing taste for all things Italian and were inspired in no small part by the Renaissance predilections of Francis I (1494–1547), who saw Italy and the ancient world as the ideal aesthetic model. The architecture of the new châteaux and their garden settings, with their luxurious and often festive magnificence and scale, are testaments to their owners' zest for life. The freedom of design gives off an air of "make-believe" that sets these pleasure palaces apart in our imagination (Fig. 23).

This new enthusiasm for the antique world of Greece and Rome following the Italian example permeated every aspect of French culture, led by the "second Italian invasion" of artists and humanists of Francis's court at Fontainebleau. Equally important were the new books and engravings illustrating *"la bonne maniera italienne"* that were beginning to circulate widely in France and open the eyes of French artists and landscape architects to the style of the late Quattrocento. The works of Vitruvius, Alberti, and Filarete introduced an entirely new vocabulary of architectural theory to French architects, and this was reinforced by the arrival of the Italian artists Giovanni Battista Rosso, Primaticcio, Giacomo da Vignola, and Serlio at Fontainebleau in the 1520s and 1540s. With the death of Rosso in 1540, Primaticcio became the head of all artistic activity at Fontainebleau, creating what Vasari was to call a "new Rome." In its assimilation of local traditions, combined with the more sophisticated heritage imported from another and older culture, Vasari's appraisal of French art is particularly apt. At the same time, it became mandatory for young French artists and humanists, who would later exert a crucial influence on the direction of the French Renaissance including garden design, to study in Rome, where they could actually explore the remains of the classical world. De l'Orme, du Cerceau, and Jean Bullant measured and analyzed the ancient, melancholy ruins buried in vegetation and decay, attempting to grasp the essential elements of classical architecture with a greater accuracy than even Alberti and the Florentine humanists of a century earlier (Fig. 24).

Leon Battista Alberti (1404–1472) was the first of the modern architectural theorists to consider the essential character of the garden as an integral part of a physical setting for a villa, and as an extension of its creator's attitude toward life. Alberti's Latin treatise, first published in Florence in 1485 and translated into French by Jean Martin in 1553 as *L'architecture et art de bien bastir,* was, of course, the theoretical cornerstone of Renaissance architecture. The elaborate French folio edition with woodcuts copied from the 1550 Florentine edition was dedicated to Henri II, and its courtly elegance was heightened by the long opening epitaph by the poet Pierre Ronsard. Alberti had drawn his cool, disciplined ideas more from the surviving fragments of the ancient texts of Vitruvius than from the mysterious, romantic ruins themselves. Since no treatise on classical gardens or landscape theory had survived and antique garden remains were nonexistent, the Renaissance humanist, wishing to recreate a garden along ancient lines, was largely dependent on literary descriptions of the Golden Age.

Alberti took as his model the account of the gardens of Pliny the Younger, but in Alberti's austere and utterly objective language it is difficult to relate the Italian architect's interpretation of classical design to the exuberant, hedonistic French gardens of the sixteenth century. "I, for my part, hate everything that favors of Luxury or Profusion," Alberti wrote, but it was a puritan righteousness that found little support at the court at Fontainebleau.[10] Nor, for that matter, does his definition of "beauty to be a harmony of all the parts" or his demand that "the architect ought to keep his main lines in strict proportion and regularity" seem to govern the uncoordinated composition of the earliest garden plan of Fontainebleau that had evolved a century after Alberti's treatise.

Despite the appeal to the French of Alberti's rational, abstract, mathematical language devoid of poetic imagination, the popular contemporary work of Fra Francesco Colonna's allegorical garden fantasy, *Hypnerotomachia Poliphili*, was equally enticing, and tended to balance Alberti's strictly intellectual attraction. The caprice and imagery of Colonna's narrative and the growing body of classical literature, with its nostalgic descriptions and allusions to luxurious gardens of the past, may well have altered the very perception of nature and of the garden in the sixteenth century (Fig. 25).

The racy, idiosyncratic blending of mythology, history, and legend into French art and architecture gave the school of Fontainebleau its special vitality. Ovid's poetry had become the new religion, and his art of love was usually practiced in a garden. The decoration of the palace was rich with allegorical references to the ancient world of Greece and Rome, and the same themes were beginning to appear in the decorations of the garden. One of the functions of the Renaissance garden was to stimulate and nourish the mind of the visitor, as well as his senses, and to remind him of the connection between the garden's creator and the legendary classical past by means of allegorical associations. Thus the antique gods, goddesses, nymphs, and satyrs in bronze and marble moved among the ornamental plantings and waterways of French gardens, finding there a most congenial asylum where they could enjoy their often reprehensible pleasures and unconscionable deceits.

The gods of the ancient world had actually survived all along within the culture and art of the Middle Ages, though their means of survival were at times ingenious and disguised. Their reappearance in various original classic forms or copies for villa and garden decoration in the fifteenth and sixteenth centuries was only their most visual and authentic manifestation.

When the Italians first began to discover large quantities of ancient sculpture beneath their gardens and fields, the sheer quantity made it impossible to accommodate these treasures in their houses, so they were moved outdoors to terraces and arbors to form garden museums. In his dialogue *De Nobilitate,* written in 1483, the humanist Poggio described the antique statues he had placed in his garden. Later his collection passed into the hands of Cosimo de'Medici, who also loved to use sculpture as a garden ornament. When Lorenzo de'Medici built his casino and laid out the gardens on the Piazza San Marco, he moved quantities of sculpture into the loggia and garden arbors, where they were to serve as models for his drawing school.

Rome, too, adopted the fashion of creating garden museums in the early sixteenth century, led principally by the example of Pope Julius II, who had started collecting sculpture for his garden even before he was Pope. By 1523, his collection in the Belvedere included the *Laocoön,* the *Apollo,* the *Venus Felix,* the *Cleopatra,* and two colossal figures of the river Gods of the Nile and Tiber.[11] The Pope's famous collection was to become a mecca for French artists working in Rome, and so it was inevitable that Francis I should commission Primaticcio to bring back from Rome —along with a contemporary marble *Hercules* by Michelangelo—four casts of classical sculpture in 1540 to enlarge the modest royal collection of a few ancient works. Vignola, who had arrived with Primaticcio on his return from Italy in 1541, together with other Bolognese craftsmen, immediately set about casting bronzes from the Roman copies for the Queen's gardens *"che fece in ditto luogo quasi una nuova Roma."*[12] Antique sculpture was also used to decorate the grotto at Meudon.

The splendid and festive style of Fontainebleau permeates the cult of the garden and nature during the reigns of Francis I and Henri II and has been portrayed in engravings, paintings, and in the series of tapestries illustrating the legend of Vertumnus and Pomona. This legend is played out on the stage of a magnificent garden where the architecture and decoration are intricately interlaced with nature itself, creating a rich, mossy texture wherein the slender, elegant figures move through an ideal garden world of clipped hedges and green tunnels —temples of living foliage and flower beds punctuated with urns and sculpture.

The young poets at Fontainebleau, like the artists and architects, were also acquiring a thorough knowledge of the classics and the literature of Homer, Pindar, Virgil, Ovid, and Horace. Their poetic imagination reflected a new spirit where nature, garden scenery, and the mythology of the past were interwoven into verses that complemented the new tapestries, frescoes, sculpture, and the royal gardens themselves. Their songs actually accompanied the reenactment of antique adventures beside the canals and in the pools of Fontainebleau (Fig. 26).

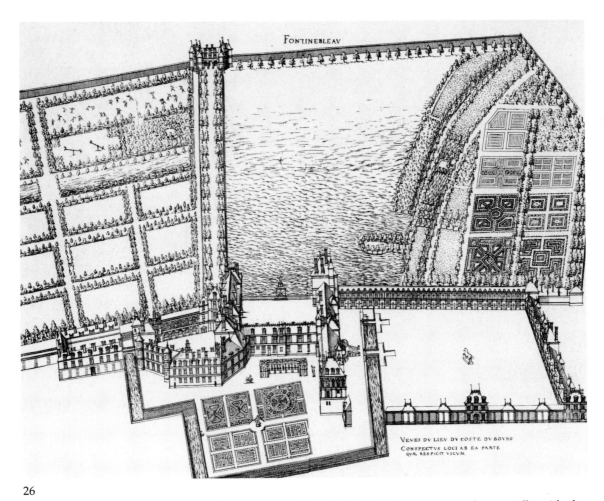

FONTINEBLEAV

VEVES DV LIEV DV COSTE DV BOVRG
CONSPECTVS LOCI AB EA PARTE
QVÆ RESPICIT VICVM

26

As that most sensual and visual century progressed, especially with the arrival of Catherine de'Medici, the great festivals of the French court grew in richness and splendor, fostered by Italianate artistry and the theatrical spirit of the French musical humanist movement led by the court poet Pierre Ronsard. Poets, architects, painters, sculptors, and musicians were brought together to create spectacles to awe and impress foreigners with the power of the court, to stir the loyalty of Frenchmen and, after the political and religious crisis deepened in the second half of the sixteenth century, to subtly express the political policy of the state. The court festival, especially as it was masterminded by Catherine, often provided an opportunity to bring together opposed factions, turning their "real conflicts into a chivalrous pastime."[13]

As these extravaganzas became more complex in scale and design, larger spaces were needed within the garden where the existing architectural elements of terraces, lakes, canals, fountains, wide walks, and sculpture were incorporated into the theatrical setting for these temporary productions. In the seventeenth century, as we shall see, this particular function of the royal gardens at Versailles would be elevated to an even more intense public policy that would profoundly affect the nature of garden design itself.

Two drawings by Antoine Caron represent festivals staged in the gardens of Fontainebleau and the Tuileries in the 1570s. Their translation into the magnificent Valois tapestries conveys in their sumptuous detail "the strange and dazzling world," in the words of Frances Yates, of French festival life staged in the idealized *capriccio* setting of a French sixteenth-century garden.[14] Without the presence of

27

the monarch, the magnificence of the costumed court, the horses and chariots, and the glittering barges on the canals, no latter-day restoration could ever revive within those gardens the original dramatic, animated quality of ritual, nor that exuberance so sadly missing in the empty, often melancholy twentieth-century re-creations.

In the Fontainebleau fête, the court and its guests are gathered around the great artificial lake in front of the *jardin de fontaine,* where a mock naval battle is being staged. In the middle, defenders in classical costumes resist the attackers, wildly maneuvering their Roman galleys, to the delight of the spectators. This particular fête has not been identified, but there are records of water tableaux being staged on the canals at Fontainebleau in 1564 where the Sirens sang warm songs of greetings to Charles IX. Neptune floated by in a car drawn by seahorses while Ronsard's lines were sung to music (Fig. 27).

The second drawing by Caron is apparently related to the fête organized for the reception of the ambassadors of Poland, who had come to Paris in August of 1573 to offer the crown of Poland to Catherine de'Medici's son, Henri. The *festin* contributed by the Queen Mother was actually staged in a temporary theater in the Tuileries and included music, dancing, and poetry. In the famous French *ballet de cour,* sixteen nymphs representing the provinces of France were carried in on an artificial rock formation (Fig. 28). Caron's drawing has removed the theater walls so that we see the two central parterres with the arms of France on one side and that of the Queen Mother on the other, flanked by two statues guarding the walk. The garden itself has been brought onto the stage, and the *rocher* setpiece seen at the left corner of the drawing with its nymphs presided over by Apollo seated on the pinnacle is an artificially created "rock of the muses" that may have actually been designed by Bernard Palissy, the ebullient garden theorist turned stage designer. Like the grotto, Palissy's simulated piece of rustic nature—represented by the rock juxtaposed against the formal, sculptural intensity of the layout of the garden—is typical of the mannerist confrontations between naturalism and idealization, illusion and reality. In grottos, hermitages, nymphaeums, and theaters—both temporary and permanent—these architectural fantasies introduced that necessary element of contrast upon which all gardens depend. They perpetuated in the Renaissance garden a capricious, romantic, medieval spirit that contradicted the calculated, rational order which had so clearly begun to dominate the direction of French garden design.

28

Caption Notes *Chapter II*

Fig. 12—Façade of *Grotte des Pins* at Fontainebleau. (Cabinet des Estampes, Bibliothèque Nationale)

Fig. 13—*Grotte de Meudon*. Silvestre's drawing shows the *Grotte* in its finished state surveying a seventeenth-century garden, but its earlier theatrical setting is plainly evident. From the terrace, the Seine and Paris beyond gave a fine prospect. (Cabinet des Dessins, Musée du Louvre)

Fig. 14—Interior of the *Grotte de Wideville*. Even though it is early seventeenth century, its fanciful, preserved interior gives some idea of grotto interiors of the century before, such as *La Batie d'Urfé*, c. 1551. (Photograph from *Jardins Français Crées à la Renaissance*, by Alfred Marie).

Fig. 15—Detail of garden fountain engraved by Jean le Pautre, one of the most talented French draftsman-designers of the seventeenth century. His theatrical use of an enormous natural boulder comes out of the *mise-en-scene* of court festivals and masques of the century before. A similar fountain form existed at Saint-Germain-en-Laye in the sixteenth century. (Dumbarton Oaks Garden Library)

Fig. 16—Stage set by Silvestre after Torrelli. Although it is not certain, the garden in the background may be real with the stage rocks and trees placed in front of it. (Metropolitan Museum of Art)

Fig. 17—*Maison Blanche* at Gaillon engraved by du Cerceau. A long, tree-lined *allée* connected the pleasure retreat with the main garden. (Dumbarton Oaks Garden Library)

Fig. 18—Detail of *Maison Blanche*. (Cabinet des Estampes, Bibliothèque Nationale)

Fig. 19—*Chantilly*. Du Cerceau's plan is the earliest view of the old fortress of triangular plan, transformed for Giullaume de Montmorency in 1530. (Dumbarton Oaks Garden Library)

Fig. 20—*Dampierre*. Du Cerceau's drawing differs in many details from the later published engraving. This is notably evident in the designs of the ornamental parterres nearest the château and in the two upper beds which are seen laid out as the *potager* in the drawing. In the engraving these squares have been given indifferent ornamentation. A narrower canal to the right of the long basin is also indicated in the engraving. (British Museum. Photograph courtesy of the Conway Library, Courtauld Institute of Art)

Fig. 21—*Vallery*. Again, du Cerceau's drawing is richer in detail and at variance with the better known published engraving in *Les Plus Excellents Bastiments*, where only six ornamented compartments are shown on either side of the basin instead of eight. (British Museum. Photograph courtesy of the Conway Library, Courtauld Institute of Art)

Fig. 22—*Vallery*. Garden with its complex water system can be seen on the left in du Cerceau's drawing. Like Blois and Gaillon, the garden space is completely separated and unrelated to the architecture. By contrast, the early Italian Renaissance villas such as Lorenzo de'Medici's Poggio a Cajano looked out into the surrounding gardens and countryside over which the lord in his house had mastery and aesthetic communion. (British Museum. Photograph courtesy of the Conway Library, Courtauld Institute of Art)

Fig. 23—Garden Pavilion, *Montargis*. The château was given to the daughter of Louis XII, Renée de France, in 1560. The complete plan of the gardens, which radiated out on three sides of the château complex, can be seen in du Cerceau's engraving in *Les Plus Excellents Bastiments de France*. In another view of the gardens, du Cerceau shows members of the court promenading through the grounds. (Dumbarton Oaks Garden Library)

Fig. 24—Anonymous drawing from a sixteenth-century French sketchbook showing reconstructed ancient sites in Italy. (Photograph courtesy of the Conway Library, Courtauld Institute of Art)

Fig. 25—Garden fountain from *Hypnerotomachia*. (Dumbarton Oaks Garden Library)

Fig. 26—*Fontainebleau*. Du Cerceau's engraving when compared with his drawing of Fontainebleau should be taken with caution, but the basic setting around the artificial lake was well established and can still be seen. Notice what appears to be an exercise yard in the upper left corner. The marshy ground made not only the lake, but the network of tree-lined canals a necessity. The flower garden, divided into four squares, was dedicated to Diana, whose statue stood among the flowers and ornamented beds north of the castle. (Dumbarton Oaks Garden Library)

Fig. 27—Water tableau on the lake at *Fontainebleau*. This drawing by Antoine Caron probably dates from 1573. (National Gallery of Scotland, Edinburgh)

Fig. 28—*Festival for the Polish ambassadors*. The drawing by Antoine Caron, like Fig. 27, was used for the later designs of the Valois Tapestries. Catherine de'Medici's reception of the ambassadors from Poland came exactly one year after the fatal festivities she celebrated at the Navarre-Valois wedding on the eve of the ghastly massacre of Saint Bartholomew. The garden setting for the Queen Mother's fête is symbolically accurate, although the actual scene depicted here took place in a temporary theater in the gardens. Bernard Palissy, the garden designer, may have created Mont Parnassus on the left. The royal emblems have been worked into the parterres with tall trees planted in the corners. (Fogg Art Museum, Harvard University)

III. Premises of Order

1. Stressing Harmony

"It is a commendable and seemly thing," Charles Éstienne, the Parisian doctor (1504–1564) wrote in *La Maison Rustique*, "to behold out of a window manie acres of ground . . . (of) comely proportions, handsome and pleasant arbors, and, as it were Closets, delightful borders of Lavender, Rosemarie, Boxe and other such like."[1] Looking at a garden and its intricate compartments from the vantage point of the window of a house, as the doctor recommended, or from one of its porticos, was by no means the conventional or even possible view of the fragmented garden spaces in the first half of the sixteenth century. At Amboise, Blois, Gaillon, and even at Catherine de'Medici's Chenonceaux, the gardens were created as separate, self-contained units and placed at some distance from the château with no spatial or visual relationship between the architecture and its setting. As the garden was extended, new spaces were simply added as separate modules and usually isolated by walls or by deploying the spaces at different levels as one sees, for example, at Gaillon.

Alberti, in his treatise written before 1450, had insisted on a total governing system of related harmonious proportions encompassing the setting as well as the building itself. Order, proportion, symmetry, and distribution were to be the informing principles of all architecture, to which nothing could be added or removed without destroying the overall harmony and beauty.

The essentially conservative use of earlier building sites and existing structures, however, in the first part of the sixteenth century prevented the classical architectural rules so eagerly employed by the Italians in their new country villas from being applied to the French gardens expanding from the center of remodeled medieval castles. The elevated walks and terraces did, however, begin to alter the spectator's perspective with glimpses of distant views that generated the possibilities of a new system for a site plan that was more spacious and unified. Sebastiano Serlio's strict, formal plan of Ancy-le-Franc, begun in 1546, imposed the new rules of abstract unity and axial symmetry over château and garden (Fig. 29). The emphasis on regularity created by the central axis dividing the parterres and running through the château would, of course, become a fundamental principle of French gardens during the following century. Serlio's imaginative use of the old defensive terrace of the medieval moat surrounding the château as an ornamental wall for viewing the flat garden space was also an important innovation.

Shortly after his accession to the throne in 1547, Henri II appointed Philibert de l'Orme, who had studied and traveled in Italy, to be in complete charge of the royal buildings and gardens. For the next twelve years, de l'Orme was to be constantly employed by the King and his mistress, Diane de Poitiers.[2] On a flat plain in the bend of the Dure River some thirty-five miles southwest of Paris, the

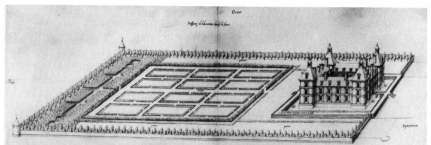

29

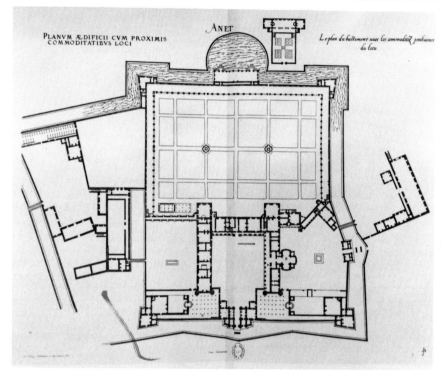

Anet

30

Anet

31

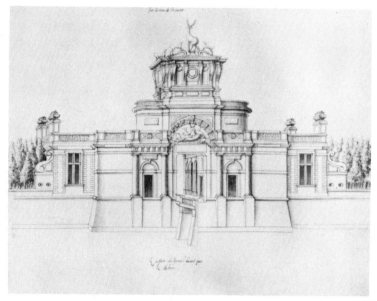

Anet

32

ambitious, well-preserved widow, seventeen years older than the King, gave the architect one of his first major commissions: to create for her *"Les Paradis d'Anet"* (Fig. 30). Again, we must turn to du Cerceau's plans to see exactly how de l'Orme conceived of this temple complex ostensibly built by Diane as a memorial to her dead husband. It was, in fact, to be a royal hunting box presided over by the King's mistress as the goddess of the chase. The image of the classical Diana ruled from the moment one stepped through the triumphal arch forming the entrance to the château. Sculpture, fountains, paintings, and tapestries incorporating the symbols of Diana gave Anet inside and out one of the most complete and consistent iconographic programs of the sixteenth century (Fig. 31 and Fig. 32).[3] In du Cerceau's perspective one can also quickly grasp the tight organization of architecture and garden space which de l'Orme had created to give Anet a sacred, mysterious quality recalling an undefiled and ceremonious past (Fig. 33).

In the courtyard and gardens five fountains can be seen in du Cerceau's engraving. The most famous, the *Diane d'Anet*, is shown in the courtyard to the left of the central entrance and is probably an allegorical portrait of Diane de Poitiers. Its cold marble poise prompted Kenneth Clark to call it a "super fashion plate" (Fig. 34). A pool is formed in the moat along the north wall recalling the mythical Diana's bath in the grove, while a bathhouse in the middle of the pool is shaped like Diana's sign of the moon and is aligned with the center of the *cour de logis* of the château. The ornamental trees planted at either side of the entrance may also evoke Ovid's account of the scene in the grove where Diana's fateful encounter with Acteon occurred, as she bathed with her nymphs.

Even though a spectator viewing the garden from a window in the central block would see "manie acres of ground of comely proportions," the overall effect is flat and centripetal, with the static parterres held within the firm pattern of intersecting walks. As Derek Clifford has correctly pointed out, Anet, with its galleried walls surrounding the garden on three sides while the château itself encloses the fourth, is essentially a medieval, inward-looking design, but nevertheless a very "refined echo of the past."[4] De l'Orme, with his earlier study of the antiquities of Rome, brilliantly translated into the curves and crescents all of the goddess's signs and attributes that were both classical and "profoundly French," in the words of Anthony Blunt. As a setting for the ritual and festivities connected with the hunt, a sport that obsessed the melancholy King, one can see in the Anet panel from the Valois tapestries how well the gardens and the

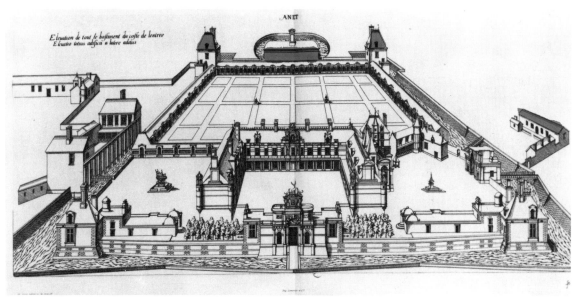

33

Anet

34

Anet

architectural backdrop worked as a well-defined theater space where music was an important element. "I have had made in the château d'Anet," de l'Orme wrote, "two little pavilions overlooking the park where may be put the players of cornets and trumpets and other instruments to give pleasure to the King and to the Princess."[5]

In order to fully appreciate the essentially conservative quality of Anet's garden, one has only to compare it with the progressive development of contemporary gardens in Italy of about the same period. Bold, unexpected perspectives combined with a confident manipulation of foliage, water, and land mass at Vignola's Caprarola and Pirro Ligorio's Villa d'Este at Tivoli, for example, were soon to point garden architecture in a new and radical direction (Fig. 35), taking full advantage of spectacular settings.

It is significant that many of the greatest Renaissance architects — Alberti, Vignola, Giuliano da Sangallo, Guilio Romano, and Bramante—contributed to the art of landscape design as a natural extension of the architecture into the surrounding space. This role of the architect was not lost on the French architectural students in the sixteenth century who studied in Rome, where Bramante's revolutionary Cortile del Belvedere was begun in 1505 for Pope Julius II. A quick succession of major Italian gardens followed Bramante's example, with Peruzzi's Villa Farnesia in 1508–1511, the work of Vignola at the Villa Julia in 1551–1553 (coinciding almost exactly with Anet and Montceaux), the Palazzo Caprarola in 1559, and the nearby Villa Lante at Bagnaia finished in 1588. To this incomparable calendar of achievement we can add the magnificent gardens at Frascati built between 1500 and 1600 and the vast complex of the Villa d'Este built between 1550 and 1569. From these models French artists, architects, landscape gardeners, and patrons who traveled to Italy found inspiration and ideas which were to be translated over the next century and a half.

In Bramante's grandiose scheme of the Belvedere at the Vatican, the architect overcame the awkward, uneven terrain by the ingenious creation of three terrace levels connected by a succession of stairways, and it is a landmark in the history of landscape planning (Fig. 36). It is likely that it had its first impact in France on Primaticcio's design of the *Grotte de Meudon*. Another example that reflects signifi-

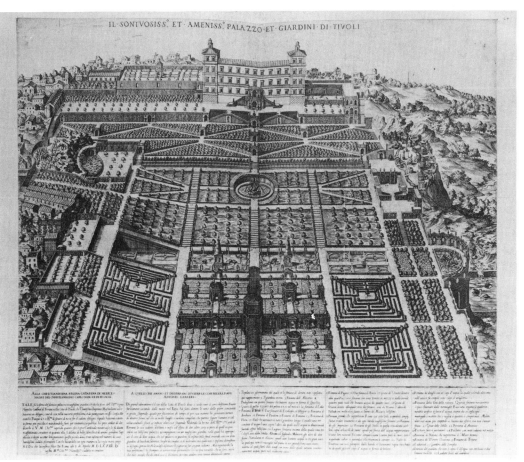

IL·SONTVOSISS.·ET·AMENISS.·PALAZZO·ET·GIARDINI·DI·TIVOLI

35

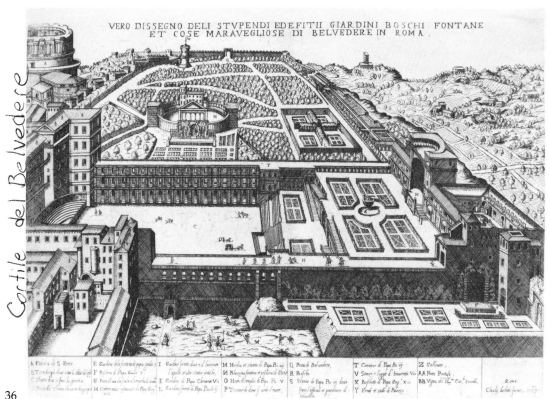

VERO DISSEGNO DELI STVPENDI EDEFITII GIARDINI BOSCHI FONTANE ET COSE MARAVEGLIOSE DI BELVEDERE IN ROMA.

36

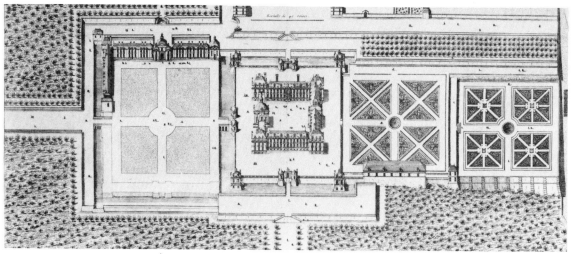

Montceaux

cant ties to Bramante's model is Montceaux, a garden begun about the same time as Meudon.

In 1547 Catherine de'Medici purchased an ancient manor house not far from Meaux, a small town just to the east of Paris. The old house was pulled down, and shortly afterwards the Queen began the construction of the new château of Montceaux on the side of the hill, placing the main axis of the gardens parallel to the hill itself (Fig. 37). It is unfortunate that du Cerceau did not leave us one of his concise birds-eye perspectives to illustrate how the two nearly equal garden spaces on successive levels below the terrace platform of the château employed a concept of organization that took unexpected advantage of the irregular terrain. Perelle's view, while distorted, does given an idea of the concept (Fig. 38). Even though the château has been reduced to a few scattered ruins, and the garden terraces returned to agriculture, one can still stand at the edge of the upper terrace and experience something of the dramatic quality in the sweep of the strong axial line running across the two flat garden levels below, leading the eye toward the distant landscape and horizon (Fig. 39 and Fig. 40).

Montceaux's earlier attribution to Primaticcio would have made a neat case to relate the initial design of the château to the transplanted Italian architect and Queen, but the history of the château is more complicated.[6] Rosalys Coope has persuasively argued the case for Philibert de l'Orme and later Salomon de Brosse as the principal architects. But even if Catherine had been willing to employ de l'Orme, her rival's architect, it is difficult to relate the advanced layout of Montceaux to de l'Orme's garden design for Diane de Poitiers at Anet.

Israel Silvestre's view of the gardens dated 1673 incorporates the later additions that Henri IV made for Gabrielle d'Estrées and the changes carried out by Marie de'Medici. However, if we can accept the basic form of the layout as dating from Catherine's purchase of Montceaux in the 1550s, then the open, axial organization that integrates the forecourt, the château terrace, and the two gardens spread out in more or less equally divided modules on different levels, is indeed advanced and implies a strong liaison with contemporary Italian landscape garden theory and practice.

The heavy wall of trees along the upper side of the two gardens is an effective architectonic massing of plant material reminiscent of the five rows of trees tightly grouped on the roof terrace at either side of the entrance to Anet, but on a much larger scale. At Montceaux, the raised trees forcefully extend and balance the line of the buildings and frame one side of the forecourt to the left of the main entry gate.

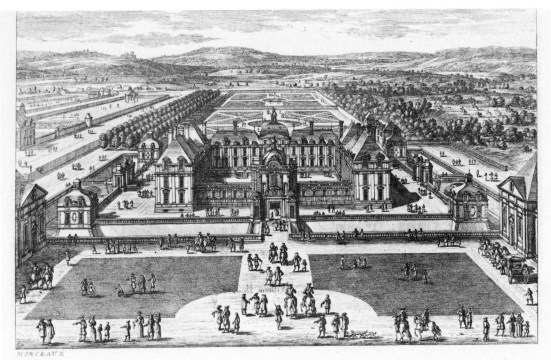

38

MONCEAUX

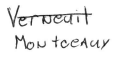

MONTCEAUX

39

Verneuil

Montceaux

40

A further stage in the Renaissance development of the French garden ideal was reached at Verneuil and Charleval and attributed to du Cerceau. Both have completely disappeared, but du Cerceau's projects, probably dating from 1568, give us an idea of their triumphant combining of architecture with the natural elements of water and plant material into a unified and magnificent work of landscape art.

Begun in 1558 by Philippe de Boulinvilliers on an irregular site above the Oise River, it is not certain how much of what we see in du Cerceau's views of Verneuil was actually carried out, although Louis Huygens, the Dutch diplomat traveling in France a century later in 1655, was impressed with the surviving garden (Fig. 41).[7] Again, stressing the harmony created by a strong central axial plan we have already seen in the Roman Renaissance gardens, there are a number of similarities between Verneuil's plan and those of the Villa d'Este, as both Naomi Miller and David Coffin have pointed out. Bramante's Belvedere and the Villa Lante, with their celebrated use of different levels, are also obvious antecedents.

From the upper terrace, laid out in sixteen geometric beds centered on a monumental shell fountain as a focal point, one descended by double stairs into a second parterre on a lower level which was flanked by tree gardens heavily massed on either side. The cross axis established by the tree parterres was reinforced by two parallel canals of equal width. The role of water at Verneuil in the fountains, the canals, and the moat was important, and its shimmering reflections must have lightened the massive presence of the architecture of the château and its heavy military retaining walls.

The relentless order of the garden at Charleval sends the mind reeling down its ordered walks and along the ornamental canals, where nature is hypnotized by an almost totalitarian vision of a Renaissance paradise on earth. Set apart from nature by water on all four sides, the plan is a radical attempt to impose an obsessive harmony that probably reflected a deep longing to escape the treacherous, chaotic world of the party divisions and religious wars that had torn France apart.

The plans of Charleval probably never advanced much beyond the plates reproduced in *Les Plus Bastiments de France,* for his patron Charles IX died shortly after work had started (Fig. 42). Yet, in its ordered expanse of meticulously controlled spaces, Charleval points toward the formal splendor that would swallow up nature in the royal gardens of Versailles in the seventeenth century. The enormous space within the base court was five hundred feet square and could have actually held the entire château of Chambord. The complex of buildings and courts covered more than thirty acres, and the garden is scaled accordingly. The circular space that terminates the garden in du Cerceau's plan was in fact to be only the center of the garden scheme twice as large as the engraved portion.

Looking out from inside the enormous banqueting hall that spanned the entire garden site of the château, with its rows of double columns dappled by the light reflected from the water of the wide canal below, the central walk led to a pavilion within a circular area surrounded by a colonade labeled "Théâtre" in du Cerceau's plan. Just what kind of ceremonial pageant or luxurious court entertainment it might have accommodated must be left to the imagination.

Even though Verneuil and Charleval followed Vitruvius's dictum that "persons of high rank who hold office" must occupy "lofty halls and very spacious peristyles, plantations and broad avenues furnished in a majestic manner," du Cerceau's châteaux and their gardens have an element of theatrical exaggeration about them that is far removed from ancient Roman palaces and villas. The harmony that unites the architecture and gardens in the sixteenth century is nevertheless a Renaissance realization of the classical ideal which both French and Italian architects worked to achieve through their control over all questions of landscape design.

Verneuil

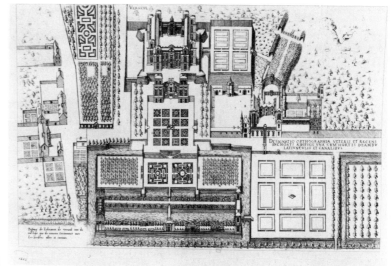

41

Charleval

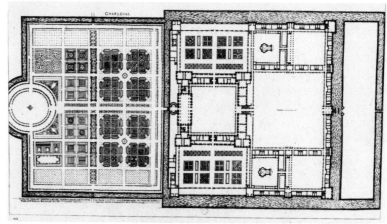

42

St. Germain-en-Laye

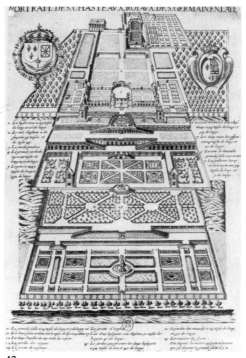

43   44

In the second half of the century, French interest in Italian garden design was further whetted by drawings and engravings of the famous gardens. Étienne du Perac's views of the Belvedere and the Villa d'Este published in 1573 were dedicated to Catherine de'Medici. On his return from Italy the artist was appointed *Grand Architect du Roy* by Henri IV, who began the development of a new château and gardens on the steep slopes of Saint-Germain-en-Laye in 1599 (Fig. 43).

Du Perac's precise role in the plan of Henri IV's garden is unclear, but the site itself is reminiscent of the Villa d'Este, and the influence of Cardinal Ippolito d'Este's gardens of "fame and beauty," long acclaimed by French admirers, can clearly be seen. An even more direct Italian source appears to be the Villa Lante, where some of the features are even more closely related to Saint-Germain.

The six levels reached in stages from the river up to the new château, which Henri had placed at the edge of the bluff with the Seine stretched below and *"un horizon a souhait pur le plaisir des yeux."*[8] The successive series of garden terraces connected with stairs, each with its own ornaments of grottos, fountains, and water pieces organized on a steep central axial line, forced the spectator to actively participate in the garden's experience by moving through it rather than merely contemplating it from a fixed viewpoint. The intricate, ceremonial choreography of controlled vistas and movement recalls Verneuil, Montceaux and the Roman temple scheme at Palestrina (Fig. 44).

The first stage next to the river was dominated by the *Fontaine du Rocher,* large water parterres, and two ornamental canals where the formal organization of the space contrasted dramatically with the natural movement of the river close by. Double stairs at either end of the terrace ascended to the next level called the *terrasse dorique,* measuring 723 feet by 332 feet.

On the landing of the stairs and on a central axis to vary one's view and movement and leading to the next terrace, a fountain surmounted with a tall figure of Mercury marked the longitudinal center of the scheme between the river and the château.

Under the terrace wall was located the famous *grottes de Orphée* and *Percée,* each richly decorated with shellworks, paintings, and statuary. Something of this strange, artificial world can still be seen in the interior of the nymphaeum at Widerville, where some of the original decorative details dating from the early seventeenth century still survive. Two more grottos with fantastic waterworks and a water organ were located immediately below the stairs leading to the terrace above and were flanked by the two chapels for the King and Queen. The grottos and fountains at Saint-Germain-en-Laye were the work of the great Florentine *fontainer* Thomas Francini—Henri IV having persuaded his Italian father-in-law to send Francini to France when the King married Marie de'Medici. Francini's hydraulic system miraculously operated the ingenious automata in the grottos and *des orques où de la Demoiselle,* and was the most complex water engineering to be seen in France (Fig. 45).

Water in the form of elaborate fountains, pools, canals, and cascades, exploiting the full emotional and intellectual range of water's visual effects, had become by the end of the sixteenth century one of the most important elements in the composition of French gardens. As the study of hydraulics and water science advanced, illustrated books on the subject proliferated, providing a catalogue of mechanical means to create sophisticated water displays of jets, fountains, automata, water organs, and other effects achieved by moving water (Fig. 46).

Salomon de Caus (1576–1616), engineer, physicist, and landscape architect, in his *Les Raisons des Forces Mouventes* explains in great detail the mechanics of moving water. In the section *"où desseignées sont plusieurs grottes et fontaines,"* de Caus lists twenty "problems" of water designs for the gardens.[9] Problem fourteen, describing an artificial mountain eighty feet high enclosed in a balustraded pond, sounds very much like du Cerceau's hermitage at Gaillon. With a reclining

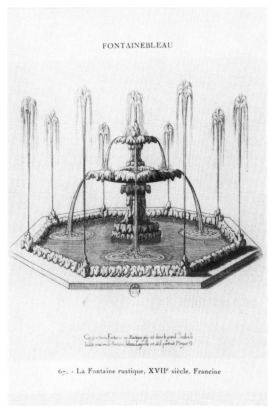

FONTAINEBLEAU

67. - La Fontaine rustique, XVIIᵉ siècle, Francine

45 &t-(GermAin-en-hAye   46   Fout

figure on top and grottos below and with Apollo, Pan, and Midas in residence, de Caus presents an image that is also similar to some of Palissy's water and garden inventions.

When Henri IV summoned the Italian engineer Francini to France in 1597 to work on the water systems in his gardens, it was an extension of the French tradition extending back to Charles VIII, when the architect-engineer Fra Giocondo was brought to Blois from Naples. Alfonso's new hydraulic system in Naples, with its aqueducts and rumbling labyrinth of buried conduits to supply the gardens and fountains, impressed the French military engineers as much as his advanced defense system of fortifications. In fact, many of the engineering skills used in Renaissance military construction were the same as those required in building gardens. Architects and engineers who worked on fortresses easily applied their skills in moving earth, building retaining walls, and constructing the terraces, pools, and avenues of landscape gardens.

It is no accident that Giuliano da Sangallo, Bramante, and other major architects of the Renaissance worked on both military fortifications and garden design problems, as well as urban planning. The steady advance of artillery firepower increasingly defined the open spaces around Renaissance fortifications. Streets and squares were viewed as potential fields of fire cutting through the medieval maze of buildings that had formerly surrounded the fort. In his study of Renaissance military engineering, George Hersey has shown how this pattern of ever-increasing firepower opened up the urban plan, creating a geometric series of consciously linked spaces where streets, alleys, and squares were seen as fields of cannon fire.[10] The same concept of space in the avenues and connected spaces within the Renaissance garden consciously drew on this pattern, which had also profoundly influenced the planning of cities.

47

The earth works, terraces, and hydraulic systems that Henri IV utilized in building the gardens of Saint-Germain-en-Laye were as startling to the contemporary eye as some of the enormous fortifications he had constructed during the religious wars of the previous decades. The King was first and foremost a military leader, which made it natural for him to organize the enormous work at Saint-Germain using the same skill and command required to build a fortress. The terrace retaining wall of Saint-Germain's garden, in fact, has the massive grandeur of a Roman fortification (Fig. 47).

Undoubtedly Henri's Florentine queen, Marie de'Medici, also had much to do with advancing those Italian garden ideas which began to appear in the King's *"jardins suspendus de Babylone"* above the Seine. The use of elaborate parterres of Italian inspiration, which Olivier de Serres said "spoke in letters of the alphabets, mottoes, sign manuals and armorial bearings," had been a steadily developing feature of French garden design throughout the century (Fig. 48).[11] Charles Éstienne's *La Maison Rustique* first appeared in Latin before being translated into French in 1572 by Jean Liebault; it provided designs and detailed instructions for laying out different types of garden compartments and geometrically patterned beds.

Olivier de Serres's great work called *La Théâtre d'agriculture et mesnage des champs* and published in 1600 was dedicated to Henri IV. It dealt essentially with practical problems of agriculture, although de Serres recommended the use of one of the four divisions of the kitchen garden for flowers which are "more for pleasure than for profit," though clearly the vegetable, medicine, and fruit plantations are more important. He praised the pleasure garden and mentioned the recent work of the royal gardener Claude Mollet. He also did not object to the introduction of "statues, columns, pyramids, obelisks and similar pieces of marble porphry and other precious materials, the richness of whose various colors renders the garden most magnificent."[12]

Some of the parterre designs reproduced in de Serres's work were actually taken from plans by Claude Mollet, who was commissioned by Henri IV in 1595 to lay out the parterres in various royal gardens including Saint-Germain-en-Laye. Mollet's success as a skilled designer of relatively traditional patterns of compartments drew him to Fontainebleau and Montceaux and later to the Tuileries, where, as chief gardener, he worked with Pierre Le Nôtre, head of another family of professional gardeners. When Mollet died in 1648, his post at the Tuileries was taken by Pierre's grandson, André.

48 St. Germain-en-Laye

Ceiling deco
by duCereAu 49

Broderie
50

In his book *Théâtre des plans et jardinages,* Claude Mollet claimed that he had been the first to introduce the *parterre de broderie* on the inspiration of Étienne du Pérac, who had imported the idea from Italy. The *parterre de broderie* was to have a major effect on French garden designs. The delicate, symmetrical patterns of arabesque, scrolls, and palmettes united the small geometric compartments into an overall plan, filling the flat spaces of French landscape schemes. *Broderie* patterns, as the name itself suggests, were drawn from textile designs, but other sources such as architectural decorations of ceiling and walls and even the elaborate borders of illuminated manuscripts of the fourteenth and fifteenth centuries are related to the new embellishments (Fig. 49 and Fig. 50). Colored stones or clay were used to enhance the green outlines of the plants' filigreed design.

Alexandre Francini's large view of Fontainebleau made in 1614 shows the great changes that Henri IV had initiated in the gardens (Fig. 51). The front of the *cour de la fontaine,* the great island-fortress garden projecting into the lake and begun in 1594–1595, is intricately decorated in the new *broderie* style. In Francini's perspective it looks like a vast Persian rug floating on the water. Large-scale designs have also been set out in beds on either side of the recently installed canals, which focus on the famous Tiber fountain placed at the intersection. Tiber, like Neptune at Saint-Germain-en-Laye, a god of water, often presided over the garden to celebrate that element's importance, a tradition extending back to classical times when Tiber and his brother were worshipped as an unfailing source upon which life itself depended.

The two gardens that Henri IV loved—Fontainebleau and Saint-Germain-en-Laye—could not differ more in their designs, due to the contrast of their respective sites. The relationship of the Renaissance garden to its surroundings is important, even crucial. French garden theorists of the sixteenth century, such as du Cerceau and de l'Orme all wrote on the problem of choosing a garden site, but often it was largely a question of the will of the builder. Henri was to lavish enormous amounts of money and energy transforming both difficult sites, one on the side of a steep hill, the other in a flat, marshy plain, and with naturally contrasting results that challenge any theory that sees a deep general siting pattern running through the major French gardens of the period.

Claude Mollet's book did not appear until four years after his death in 1652, and thus his influence during his lifetime was due to the design innovations he actually carried out, rather than to recognition as a theorist dealing with the fundamentals of garden aesthetics. It is in Jacques Boyceau's great work *Traité du jardinage,* where a rigorous intellectual approach to the subject first raises gardening to an art, as his biographer Franklin Hazelhurst has put it.

Little is known about Boyceau's early training beyond the fact that he had a distinguished military career during the Protestant Wars. A staunch Huguenot, Boyceau was recognized by Henri IV as a capable leader of deep intellect who shared the King's enthusiasm for gardening—"who himself planted and grafted," to quote one of his admirers.[13] Boyceau nevertheless understood the importance of the professional training of gardeners, and recommended a study program of geometry, draftsmanship, architecture, and aesthetics, along with a practical background of horticultural science which the young gardener was to learn as an apprentice to an older professional. It was also important for him to "work with the spade with other laborers, learning well to cultivate the earth, to bend, straighten and bind the wood for the works of relief; to trace upon the ground his design . . . to plant and clip the parterres . . . and several other particulars which comprise the embellishment of the gardens of pleasure."[14]

Boyceau's analysis of garden art, like Palissy's, began with the fundamental elements of water, earth, air, and fire, revealing a deeply religious belief in the rational workings of God through nature. While God had distinguished and separated these contrary elements, He nevertheless gave "to each an affinity and participation with others, seeing to it that they were so disposed that they were

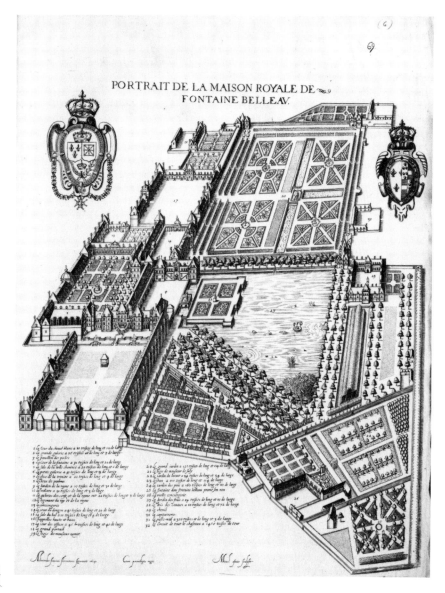

Fontainebleu

51

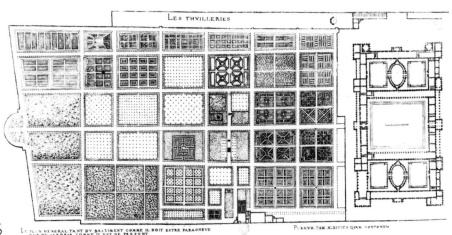

Tuileries

52

able to communicate their virtues together."[15]

In the first chapter of Book III of the *Traité du jardinage,* Boyceau applied his philosophy to the layout of the garden, declaring that "following the teachings nature gives us in so much variety, we feel the most varied gardens are the most beautiful."[16] A garden must reflect the diversity and variety of nature, which a trained landscape designer is better prepared to orchestrate than the architect who had, until this time, dominated most garden design functions. Not only parterres, *compartiments des broderies,* and water, but a wide variety of plants and trees in contrasting shapes, species, colors, and even single specimens, were to be made part of the composition. He further recommended the use of irregular terrain, a significant departure from the French predilection for level sites that often led to dullness in garden designs (Fig. 52). From the elevation of a hilly site, the visitor can grasp the entire composition "from a single point of view" recalling Charles Éstienne's pleasure in viewing the garden from the window of the house as the preferred vantage point. "You judge from this raised position," Boyceau pointed out, "the good correspondence (congruity) that exists among the parts, which all give more pleasure than would the (individual) parcels."[17]

Both Claude Mollet and Boyceau were concerned about the proper dimensions of the principal avenues, taking into account questions of perspective and optics, subjects that preoccupied painters and theatrical designers as well. The sculptured green *palissades* on each side of the *allée* must be two-thirds the width of the walk, for height itself could create negative feelings of confinement. The length and width must follow their own formula of proportion depending on whether they were covered or not. Boyceau then proceeded to analyze the very French problem of the long imperial avenues which could run a half mile in length, and where optics would reduce the exit to a pinpoint on the horizon in the distance if adjustments in proportions were not made.

Sculpture and fountains appear in the chapter "On Relief," where their chief function as vertical accents is in their location to "mark and divide up the spaces, detaining the sight, forcing the eye to stop in order to consider the relief and hence make the viewer aware of other works which these relief elements surround."[18] These cadenced accents, carefully spaced, further emphasized the ceremonial itinerary or promenade which became an integral part of the experience of the French garden. The ideal world of memory, of contemplation, and of the pleasures of the senses created in the garden and presented to the visitor had to be held together by a perfectly orchestrated score of rhythmic walks and stops.

Boyceau devoted a whole chapter to the subject of grottos. They are to be made to represent *"les autres sauvage,"* and the strangeness of their dim, interior space was to be heightened by rustic workmanship, petrified masses of stone, pebbles, and shells. The walls could also be decorated with paintings recalling ancient designs in prehistoric caves. In an increasingly ordered age the mysterious interior of the grotto which framed the visitor's view as he gazed onto a landscape completely subordinated to rational organization, gave the bright garden itself a phantom, surreal quality. The ambiguity and tension between art and nature was to be further exploited in the architecture of the grotto, where its decoration was "mixed with the polished variety, as if nature and art were vying with one another in decorating the place."[19]

No such romantic notions were proposed in André Mollet's *Le Jardin de Plaisir.* Published in French, Swedish, and German in 1651, it gave Mollet a lasting influence throughout Europe. The book, consisting of a catalogue of garden plans, is a triumph of the drafting board, and the large plates provide a variety of layouts that follow Boyceau's theories. The first plan was the prototype of the Tuileries garden, and in 1660, when André Le Nôtre was asked to redesign the old garden, he actually used Mollet's diagonally divided parterres reproduced in his book.[20] The variety of shapes in the two sets of ornamented compartments on either side of the central axis and separated by the large basins translated Boyceau's formula for avoiding dullness in the design of geometric spaces.

Mollet obviously enjoyed the Renaissance play with the senses by manipulating the garden's plants and flowers "which yield us so much delight in the variety of their Enamel Colours, pleasant odors, that there is not one of our senses which finds not itself charmed by them . . . ."[21] Trees and shrubs in the hands of a professional landscape architect were building materials, according to Mollet, to be placed and controlled according to the design's requirements. Size, shape, and color were important. For the outlines of the parterres and the "Knots in Embroidery" the easily managed box was preferred. The larger ground patterns could be formed from neatly rolled and clipped turf. Lime or beach trees were best for the main avenues and the large tree masses. Cyprus trees "cropt neatly in Pyramidal form" and kept to a height of six or seven feet could be placed between the rows of taller trees in the avenue to form a rhythmic wall at eye level.

A strict hierarchy of plant material had, by that time, been established for the pleasure garden, and common herbs or fruit trees, except as espaladed ornaments on walls, were not to be admitted. As for flowers, Mollet did little more than indicate the spaces where a variety of curious and exotic specimens could be displayed. In one of his compartments he indicated where square stones were to be laid to support flowerpots or small boxes of topiary trees. Potted orange trees could also be combined with low and exotic flowers to give diversity within harmony.

After the fall of Constantinople, European gardens were inundated with exotic new plant material sent back from Turkey by Western mercenaries who were fascinated by the strange array of Asiatic flowers they found growing in Turkish gardens. "Never before or since has there been such a sudden astonishing influx of colorful strange plants into European gardens," William Stern has written concerning this botanical revolution. ". . . Unpromising onion-like bulbs and knobbly tubers from Constantinople brought forth tulips, crown imperials, irises, hyacinths, anemones, turban ronunculi, narcissi and lilies," he continues, and their beauty was immediately disseminated by artists in paintings, engraved books, and drawings throughout the courts of Europe.[22]

From the early days of the Crusades, international traffic in botanical specimens had been a lively business, constantly enlarging the plant collections throughout Europe. At the beginning of the Renaissance, with the new humanistic interest in science, plants joined collections of "birds, court jesters, singers and foreign animals" as a fashionable princely activity.[23] At his villa, Poggio a Cajano, Lorenzo de'Medici formed a collection of specimen plants to complement his assemblage of rare birds and animals.[24] In 1545 the first public botanical garden was founded at the University of Padua, where the emphasis was on the study of plants and herbs for medicinal purposes.

In France, the scientific collection and study of plants was widely carried out in private botanic gardens, although the royal parks under the supervision of professional gardeners and horticulturists served much the same function. In 1593 Jean Robins, director of the royal gardens of the Louvre, sent a list of seeds he wanted to Ulissa Aldrovandi, the great Italian naturalist and founder of the Botanical Garden at Bologna.[25] Robins designed *compartiments de broderie* in the new fashion of du Pérac and Claude Mollet, using only foreign plants. Another passionate gardener and collector, Jean de Brancion, the Burgundian nobleman, was regularly exchanging plants in the middle of the sixteenth century with Alfonso Panza, Rector of the Gardens of Simples of the University of Ferrara.[26]

Greenhouses using solar heat or braziers were important in Northern gardens in order to protect exotic plants, and an orangery was an early part of the garden architecture at Blois. By the end of the sixteenth century they had become a standard piece of equipment. Palissy, in *The Delectable Garden*, proposed a series of winter rooms for tender plants to be hollowed out of the rock on the south and east side of the hill above the garden, carefully placed for the maximum solar heat.

André Mollet in his treatise simply considered the greenhouse a basic garden tool of the pleasure garden, although at Versailles we will see it in the form of Mansart's orangery which was elevated into one of the great pieces of architecture of the seventeenth century.

Armed with the treatises of de Serres, Boyceau, and the Mollets, and natural heirs to a long tradition of garden art on a majestic scale, French landscape architects were now ready to translate that heritage into its noblest forms. In the hands of André Le Nôtre, serving the worldly statecraft of the Sun King, a new era in the history of landscape art was about to begin.

Caption Notes *Chapter III (1)*

Fig. 29 — *Ancy-le-Franc*. Serlio's careful balancing of the formal layout in scale and harmony with the architecture was a major break with earlier French Renaissance garden planning. The strange carved-out pattern in the heavy wood has a secret Middle Eastern quality in du Cerceau's drawing and has the appearance of a waterway rather than the walk that appears in the published engraving. The axial line through the center dominates the design. (Courtald Institute)

Fig. 30 — *Anet*. Engraved plan by du Cerceau. (Cabinet des Estampes, Bibliothèque Nationale)

Fig. 31 — *Anet*. Surviving entrance gate. (Photograph by the author)

Fig. 32 — *Anet*. Drawing of original gate by du Cerceau. (British Museum)

Fig. 33 — *Anet*. Birds-eye view engraving from du Cerceau's *Les Plus Excellents Bastiments de France*. De l'Orme's garden, while enclosed, followed the lines of the architecture, giving the composition a rigorous symmetry and balance that was a departure from the older French gardens that had little or no relationship with the buildings. (Cabinet des Estampes, Bibliothèque Nationale)

Fig. 34 — *Anet*. The upper portion of the Fountain of Diana shown in du Cerceau's drawing is now in the Louvre. (British Museum)

Fig. 35 — *Villa d'Este* at Tivoli. Engraving by Étienne du Pérac. (Metropolitan Museum of Art)

Fig. 36 — *Cortile del Belvedere*. Engraving by Étienne du Pérac. (Metropolitan Museum of Art)

Fig. 37 — *Montceaux*. Silvestre's engraving dated 1673 shows the sharp drop in the elevation of the lower garden on the right, which is reinforced with a heavy retaining wall. The central axis running through the château from left to right disappeared over the garden terrace into the countryside itself, anticipating the garden structures of the seventeenth century at Richelieu, Vaux, and Versailles. The heavy architectural massing of trees in the gardens was widely used in the sixteenth century and can be seen in the views of Anet and Verneuil, Fig. 33 and Fig. 41. (British Museum)

Fig. 38 — *Montceaux*. Perelle's countryside beyond the garden is a bit extravagant, but the view from the château and upper terrace was impressive. (Collection of the author)

Figs. 39–40 — *Montceaux*. Actual view of garden ruins. (Photographs by the author)

Fig. 41 — *Verneuil*. Du Cerceau's engraving is probably only a projection, but it is one of the great garden plans of the French Renaissance. The view from the exedra overlooking the expanse of finely ornamented garden was bordered by *berceau* on one side with galleried walls along the outer walls next to the moat. (Cabinet des Estampes, Bibliothèque Nationale)

Fig. 42 — *Charleval*. Engraving by du Cerceau. On either side of the château were *giardini secreti*. (Bibliothèque Nationale)

Figs. 43–44 — *Saint-Germain-en-Laye*. The first pavilion and garden on the slope below the old château at center top was planned for court entertainments by Henri II and begun 1557. The great boulder fountain on the first level is similar to Le Pautre's design in Fig. 15. Unlike the terraced garden at Blois and Gaillon, which were isolated from one another, at Saint-Germain they are brought into unity with each other by means of the series of stairs held to the central axis running from the top down to the river's edge. (Bibliothèque Nationale)

Fig. 45 — *Saint-Germain-en-Laye. La Premier Gallérie des Grottes*. Engraved by Thomas Francini, 1599. (Photograph from *Jardins Français Crèes á la Renaissance*) (Dumbarton Oaks Garden Library)

Fig. 46 — *La Fontaine rustique, Fontainebleau*. Engraved by Thomas Francini, 1599. (Photograph from *Jardins Français Crées à la Renaissance*) (Dumbarton Oaks Garden Library)

Fig. 47 — Remaining walls of central stair of Saint-Germain-en-Laye. (Photographs by the author)

Fig. 48 — Detail of elaborately worked emblems of the gardens at *Saint-Germain-en-Laye*. These are probably by Claude Mollet. (Cabinet des Estampes, Bibliothèque Nationale)

Fig. 49 — Ceiling decorations by du Cerceau from *Les Plus Excellents Bastiments de France*. (Dumbarton Oaks Garden Library)

Fig. 50 — *Broderie* designs for parterres from Claude Mollet's *Théâtre*. The elaborate backgrounds were often filled in with colored earth or stones, while box gradually replaced the old clipped herbs in forming the complex designs. Mollet's designs at Saint-Germain-en-Laye can be seen in the detail of Fig. 48. By 1600, a great variety of plants and flowers had been introduced into French gardens. De Serres in his *Théâtre d'agriculture* filled the parterres with flowers such as violets, wallflowers, pinks. Imported foreign plants and bulbs such as tulips, lilies, and fritaleria added rich color which is lost in the garden engravings of the period. Symmetry was carried out not only in the layout but in the details of the plantation as well. Tall, sculptured trees, which can be seen in Caron's drawing of the Tuileries, still accented the corners of the parterres. Some plant collectors restricted their parterres exclusively to foreign flowers in order to create new embroidery patterns. (Dumbarton Oaks Garden Library)

Fig. 51 — *Fontainebleau*. One can see the enormous changes in garden fashions in the late sixteenth century by comparing Francini's engraving of 1614 with du Cerceau's, done forty years earlier, Fig. 25. (Royal Library, Stockholm)

Fig. 52 — *Tuileries*. It is difficult to say how much of the design shown in du Cerceau's engraving had actually been carried out at the time it was published in the second volume of *Les Plus Excellents Bastiments* in 1577. It was from the beginning an important public space with a variety of entertainments available within the formal layout, including a theater, menagerie, aviary, fish ponds, and later a restaurant. By the middle of the sixteenth century the regular symmetrical layout in France was well established where new gardens were concerned. (Cabinet des Estampes, Bibliothèque Nationale)

Veuë et Perspectiue du Parterre du Palais d'Orleans.

Perelle sculp.

Luxembourg

53

Veuë de la Caseade de Ruel.

Israel ex. Auec priuil. du Roy 6

Rueil

54

VEDVTA E PROSPETTO DEL GRAN TEATRO DELL. ACQVE DELLA VILLA ALDOBRANDINA DI BELVEDERE A FRASCATI.

Villa
Aldobrandini

55

III. Premises of Order

2. "Sweete Retirements"

When John Evelyn saw the terraces and walks of Marie de'Medici's Luxembourg garden animated with the crowds of citizens, strangers, gallants, ladies, and "meloncholy fryers," he declared that "nothing is wanting to render this palace and gardens perfectly beautiful and magnificent." After recounting its glories, he apologized for his long "discription of this paradise," but it was because of "the extraordinary delight I have taken in the sweete retirements."[27]

The Luxembourg is Jacques Boyceau's finest creation and firmly displays in its clear organization a step toward Le Nôtre's mature style of the formal garden. When Salomon de Brosse was asked to design a new palace by the widow of Henri IV, she expressed a desire to have it modeled on the Pitti Palace in her native Florence. While de Brosse produced a palace quite different from the intended Italian model, it is probable that the Queen had also urged on her garden designer, as an inspiration, the Florentine Boboli gardens laid out by Bernardo Buontalenti in the 1560s. It is equally apparent that she had little more effect upon Boyceau than upon de Brosse, for the results revealed something new in the finely orchestrated unity between the garden and architecture, and in the role of architecture to define and control the garden layout.

A comparison of the Luxembourg's bold composition with the gardens of Saint-Germain-en-Laye or of Fontainebleau demonstrates the break Boyceau had made with the endless elaborations of the gardens of the late French Renaissance. Instead of royal insignia woven into the parterres and fanciful topiary creations of heraldic beasts, water tricks and miraculous fountains to the design of Salomon de Caus, or the startling *"musqueteeres"* in Richelieu's gardens at Rueil who shot surprised visitors with a stream of water from their muskets, one is confronted with a powerful scheme of monumental dignity (Fig. 53).

When all of Marie de'Medici's land acquisitions for the new palace and gardens had been completed in 1629 and the lines of the gardens themselves established, the central axis running from the palace to the exedra to the south measured 340 meters, while the transverse axes were over 800 meters. This uncharacteristic emphasis given to the transverse axes rather than the central vista may be due, in part, to the recalcitrant monks whose monastery blocked the Queen's path of development to the south. But Hamilton Hazelhurst's excellent study of the Luxembourg pinpoints a similar plan for the Boboli gardens, suggesting that Boyceau may have followed the Italian precedent in order to placate the Queen's strong Florentine impulses. Actually a precedent for running the main axis parallel to the château rather than at right angles can be seen in du Cerceau's plan of Anet where the placing of the exedra is also similar, and could have been a source for Boyceau's layout.[28]

A striking feature of the Luxembourg was Boyceau's great embroidered parterre, "so rarely designed and accurately kept cut that the *embroiderie* makes a wonderful effect to the lodgings which front it," Evelyn noted. Surrounded on three sides by a double terrace for viewing, the parterre below appeared to slope upward slightly toward the large exedra space, an illusion that relieved the flat, dull topography. The parterre itself was formed by a series of units in a variety of geometric shapes, and the straight exterior lines of the garden contrasted with the rich magnificence of the finely sculptured green relief patterns inside.

The walks of the Luxembourg "are exactly fair, long and variously descending," Evelyn wrote, after he had passed along the *allées* of limes, elms, and hornbeam hedge which had matured since they had been set out fifteen years before his visit. At the east end of the main terrace running across the garden front of the palace was the *grotte du Luxembourg*. It was, in fact, a fountain, although its façade is strikingly close to the grotto at Wideville built about the same time. A heavy palisade of tall trees enclosed the parterre terraces, framing the view from the palace and increasing the overall architectural unity of the space, giving scale and measurability to the composition.

Fountains and pools provided the necessary accents and variety Boyceau was later to specify in his *Traité*. Thomas Francini, *Intendant général des jardins et fontaines de Royne, sa mere,* was employed to design the garden's waterworks and to work with de Brosse on the great *l'aqueduc d'arcueil* which was to bring the water from the Rungis to the fountains.

At about the same time that the Queen Mother was assembling and building her royal domain of the Luxembourg, her rival for power, Cardinal Richelieu, was preparing his own pleasure grounds at Rueil some five miles west of Paris. Traveling in his red and gold litter carried by eighteen men, the Cardinal would retreat from the capital to his gardens, to spend hours there in the solitude of a small island built in the middle of the lake.

The gardens of Rueil, begun in the early 1630s, were profuse in their variety of grottos, incredible fountains, and water architecture of basins and canals, although the château remodeled by Jacques Lemercier in 1635–1636 was relatively modest. The gardens were created by Jean Thiriot from designs by Lemercier.[29] One fountain shot water sixty feet into the air through a copper basilisk and oscillated to form a moving arch. Rueil's grotto was a large and "very rare" extravagance of elaborate "shell-work in the shape of satyrs, and other wild fancies," according to John Evelyn. "In the middle stands a marble table, on which a fountain plays in the divers forms of glasses, cups, crosses, fans, crowns, etc. Then the fountaineer represented a shower of rain from the top, two extravagant musketeers shot us with a stream of water from their musket barrels . . . " Nearby was the artificial cascade we see in Silvestre's engraving (Fig. 54) and vividly described by Evelyn as it rolled "down a very steepe declivity, and over the marble steps and basins, with an astonishing noyse and fury; each basin hath a jetto in it, flowing like sheetes of transparent glasse, especially that which rises over the greate shell of lead, from whence it glides silently downe a channell thro' the middle of a spacious gravel walke terminating in a grotto."[30]

The extravagance of Richelieu's cascade was a spectacle in tune with the fashionable water-animated creations which began to reach new forms of artistry in Bernini's Rome at the same time. Man-made cascades had become fashionable in the sixteenth century in Italy, among which the mock rustic falls at Tivoli (1567–1568) exuberantly simulating rugged nature were the most famous. The boulders of Tivoli's cascades contrasted dramatically with the architectural cascade at the Villa Aldobrandini (1603–1604) and reflected a basic disagreement concerning an acceptable model to follow where "nature" was involved (Fig. 55). A close reading of Vitruvius's theory of the evolution of architecture from the primitive cave and hut to buildings with the recognized qualities of architecture in the full sense of the word, examples of order, proportion, and symmetry, argued against the "natural"

Veue de la vielle Grotte de Ruel.

Israel Silvestre delin.   *Perelle sculp.*

Rueil

56

Veue de la Grotte du Jardin de Ruel, et d'vne partie du Canal et Bassins.

Israel Silvestre delin.   *Perelle sculp.*   66

Rueil

57

school. According to Vitruvius, nature, with all its imperfections and unpredictable qualities, should not serve as a literal architectural model, for it would fail to display man's superior reason and skill. The problem of finding an acceptable style for grottos as well as cascades could be clearly seen in the two different types at Rueil, one "natural," craggy, and primitive in form and the other classical and architectonic (Fig. 56 and Fig. 57).

The progeny of the classic, architectural cascades of Italy appeared in seventeenth- century France at Rueil, Saint-Cloud, Fontainebleau, Liancourt, and Vaux-le-Vicomte, where the Italian models were adapted to the refinements of French classicism (Fig. 58 and Fig. 59). In fact, the rustic, naturalistic grotto and cascade constructed from uncut rocks and laid in natural formation, such as at Tivoli, did not become firmly established in France until the late eighteenth century when the romantic gardens, inspired by Hubert Robert and his circle, encouraged the "picturesque" motif.

At the château de Liancourt, where an assemblage of unrelated garden constructions in an outmoded profusion of parterres, canals, and endless arbors covered the flat terrain, an adequate elevation could not be found for a fashionable

VEVE EN PERSPECTIVE DES CASCADES DE VAVX

VAUX - lA - VICOMTE

58

Veüe et perspectiue du Chateau des Jardins et Cascades de Liancourt

fecit por Aueline

LIANCOURT

59

Les nouvelles Cascades de St. Cloud.

60 SAINT cloud.

61 SAINT-Cloud

62

st. Cloud

Italian cascade. The problem was solved by building a series of terraces high enough to create an artificial fall. When the rich Gondi family arrived in France in Marie de'Medici's Italian train, they deliberately acquired high ground above the Seine at Saint-Cloud where they could build a full-scale cascade in the Italian style. An undated seventeenth-century drawing of the site shows the original *Maison de Gondi* and an adjacent cascade of monumental proportions. In 1658, however, when Philippe d'Orleans, the younger brother of Louis XIV, bought Saint-Cloud, he named Antoine Le Pautre his architect, who apparently replaced the earlier Gondi construction with the celebrated *grande cascade* that has survived (Fig. 60 and Fig. 61).[31]

Le Pautre's mighty hydraulic spectacle, completed in 1665, was modeled on Lemercier's more restrained and formal creation at Rueil. As a monumental water machine with an ingenious system designed to increase the force of the descending cataract, it was one of the most powerful garden decorations created in seventeenth-century France (Fig. 62). Its artificial character, as Le Pautre's biographer, Robert Berger, has pointed out, was emphasized by the sharply defined, boxlike space it occupies on the slope above the Seine. The cascade's sculptured form forcefully reminds the spectator even today, that the water pouring through its arched openings comes from a man-made, artificial source and is not, as Bernini might have designed it or later Herbert Robert, a stream falling naturally over living rock. The original curved basin at the bottom was enlarged by Hardouin-Mansart in 1698–1699, and a long canal was built to connect the basin with a distant pool which can be seen in Eugene Atget's photograph.

Caption Notes *Chapter III (2)*

Fig. 53 — *Luxembourg.* Perelle's view of the central parterre looking south from the palace. (Cabinet des Estampes, Bibliothèque Nationale)

Fig. 54 — *Rueil.* Unlike Saint-Cloud, the cascade at Rueil does not have a central gushing source at the top. Silvestre's engraving shows the special attention given to the placing of the monumental sculpture. (Collection of the author)

Fig. 55 — *Villa Aldobrandini.* Garden views like G.B. Falda's were widely circulated in France. (Dumbarton Oaks Garden Library)

Figs. 56–57 — *Rueil.* The rustic and classical grottos engraved by Perelle. (Collection of the author)

Fig. 58 — *Vaux-le-Vicomte.* The *Grand Cascade* engraved by Silvestre. (Cabinet des Estampes, Bibliothèque Nationale)

Fig. 59 — *Liancourt.* View of the cascade by Aveline. (Cabinet des Estampes, Bibliothèque Nationale)

Fig. 60 — *Saint-Cloud.* The title *Les Nouvelles Cascades de St. Cloud* further supports Professor Berger's conclusions regarding Le Pautre's role in their creation. (Collection of the author)

Figs. 61–62 — *Saint Cloud.* Eugene Atget's photographs c. 1900 make interesting comparisons with the seventeenth-century engravings. (Caisse Nationale des Monuments Historiques et des Sites)

III. Premises of Order

3. Garden as Theater

Like the modern theater, the garden as a unified creation appeared during the Renaissance (Fig. 63). In the search for ways to transform the real world by creating illusions of indefinitely extended space, and in the manipulation of symbols for emotional and psychological purposes, both theaters and gardens were shaped by common traditions. While the theater's physical requirements were more rigid because of the forms of drama it was designed to accommodate, there are, nevertheless, a number of similar characteristics to be found in both the theater and the gardens of the early Renaissance and, even more strikingly, their later Baroque forms.

A garden, like the theater, is a visual art. Just as the theater is an offspring of literature, the formal garden is a child of horticulture, but both are intimately related to painting, sculpture, and, of course, architecture. A common background of patterns and conventions formed out of religious belief, medieval legend, classical mythology, national history, and allegorical fancy was shared by the designers of gardens and of theaters, who also employed the artistic vocabularies of the painter, the sculptor, or the designer of tapestries.

The discovery of the rules of linear perspective was to have a revolutionary effect upon painting and architectural theories, including garden design. It was similarly to have no less an impact on theater decor. The perspective theater scene, creating an illusion of space and a counterfeiting of the appearance of reality, first appeared in Italy. It is easy to see the appeal that the technique would have had for landscape architects who were increasingly preoccupied with illusion and appearance, once the magic of the new scenery, often a garden setting, was revealed. Through the use and manipulation of perspective, not only a new plan for the stage, but a new ideal for the stage designer entered the theater. As George Kernodle has pointed out in his study of the metamorphosis of art into theater, "all conventional façades gave way before this triumphant principle."[32] The theory of perspective embodying the revolutionary spatial concepts of the new humanities —the philosophers, the mathematicians, as well as the scientists—was a powerful, combining force that brought a new unity to all of the visual arts, including the theater and the garden.

Italian set designers, who had pioneered the perspective stage set and had shown a special genius for all kinds of novel stage effects, were drawn to Paris, where they worked on court pageants and theatrical productions. Many of the stage devices and constructions such as temples, grottos, fountains, and sacred groves were drawn from the garden ornament vocabulary. Members of the Francini family who had been lured to France as fountaineers and garden impresarios also performed theatrical magic for Italianate entertainments and ballets. In 1610, for the music drama *Alcine,* in which the young King Louis XIII danced, the enchanted gardens of Armida were adorned with a grotto and jetting fountains created by Francini skill. Dancing knights with magic wands controlled the waters of the fountains as the dancers moved through their routine. At the cruel fête staged by Nicholas Fouquet in the garden of Vaux-le-Vicomte, Toreli, the Italian stage designer, invented rocks that broke open to reveal a bevy of nymphs, and the garden statues miraculously formed a *corps de ballet.*

While new scientific discoveries and techniques were quickly incorporated into stage productions, including supernatural effects of lightning and thunder, the so-called rules of perspective were the most fascinating to both the stage and garden designer, and both turned to the numerous books and treatises describing the basic optical laws which had to be followed to create the illusions of space on a single plane. Jean Martin's translation of Serlio's treatise on the theater, published in Paris in 1545, emphasized the importance of perspective in architectural design, and the subject was quickly picked up by his followers.

In his *Traité,* Boyceau considered the study of draftsmanship, architecture, and geometry an essential foundation for students of garden art. The theories of perspective were, of course, a part of this curriculum. Earlier, Olivier de Serres's practical instructions for laying out garden designs in his *Théâtre d'agriculture* noted that rows of trees and plants must have greater space *"par la raison de perspective"* if they were to be seen from a distance rather than at close range.

The art of perspective, especially as it was used in painting and in the theater, was based upon three principles. The first was to establish a fixed eye-point where the perspective lines would converge on a single point. For the painter, this was a fairly simple matter. For the theater it was more complex, because the exact relationship had to be established between the viewer, i.e., the audience, and the setting or stage. In the case of the garden, though there was a similarity to the problems of the theater, the problem was compounded by the sheer magnitude of the space that had to be organized and held in static balance in order to create the desired illusion.

Bramante's great garden of the Belvedere in the Vatican incorporated the new principles of perspective by establishing a fixed point of view within the garden design itself. The fact that the Belvedere included a theater program as one of its functions suggested obvious stagecraft solutions within the context of Bramante's composition. His unfettered resolution of the spatial composition of the Belvedere garden allowed the development of a new concept of space that was to dominate the future course of garden architecture. Until Bramante's design, the average Renaissance courtyard had been conceived around a focal point at the center of the composition, within the confines of four walls. But the composition of the Belvedere was planned along an axis that demanded a single point of view, forcing observation of the space from south to north in order to comprehend its aesthetic unity and cohesion. The progression of the terrace levels along the courts, receding in height as they reached the upper level of the exedra, further emphasized the analogy to painted perspective and to theater design (Fig. 64). As James Ackerman has pointed out, the out-of-doors became a conscious part of architectural planning; "a new kind of spatial expression sought to domesticate the open air."[33] The rhythmic progression of the various levels dictated by the rough terrain not only allowed Bramante to exploit its theatrical possibilities but, in his control over the space, he also celebrated that Renaissance triumph of the rationalization of nature itself in the design of the garden.

The second principle of perspective required that the entire space of the picture be unified by one picture plane and one frame. It was, in reality, a decision to treat three-dimensional space in a two-dimensional manner. It was not until the late sixteenth century that stage architects were actually able to establish this principle through the use of the proscenium arch as a means of framing and thus controlling the enclosed space. During the evolution of the proscenium in the theater, designers of the sixteenth century had experimented with three different

63

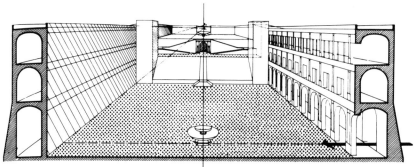

64 Cortile del Belvedere.

planes—forestage, main stage, and inner stage. Here again Bramante's lower, intermediate, and upper courts concentrated their sight lines on the exedra, following these early theater design experiments.

Similarly, the measured succession of planes parallel to the picture plane itself (which was the third principle of painted and theater perspective) can be seen again in Bramante's original scheme of the receding line of terraces between each court. The reliance on the same basic rules as those used in theater design becomes all the more apparent when one realizes that the single, unifying point of view is found not within the Cortile itself, but rather outside its frame in the window of the third floor of the Vatican palace, placing the observer (in this case the Pope) at an elevated point on a line with the exedra itself, much like the ducal box in a Renaissance theater. From this theatrical vantage point, all lines converge on the exedra itself. The view appealed to artists like du Pérac, who drew the Cortile from this vantage point and sent the engravings to the French court about the time that major work on the steep slopes of Saint-Germain-en-Laye was being planned (see Fig. 43).

The theatrical use of the techniques of perspective in France in the late sixteenth century seems to have been largely confined to the staging of Royal Entries, and to the open stages temporarily set up in streets and in palace gardens. The introduction of theatrical perspectives in the Entry can best be seen in the sequence of vistas created by the popular triumphal arches built of canvas and plaster and strategically placed along the route of the royal progress, rather like a series of large picture frames or proscenium arches.

In 1641, an important development in the history of the French stage occurred in a new production of the play *Miramé*. [34] For the first time a Parisian audience saw a stage backdrop or curtain actually painted in perspective, and used in a theater production to create the illusion of space within the confines of the stage itself. That essential element of the baroque stage was to serve as the basic scene throughout the performance of the play. However, from the standpoint of the history of French garden art, it is quite likely that the painted perspectives that John Evelyn saw in the gardens of Rueil and the Hôtel Liancourt were used as a part of the garden decor even before the technique was actually seen as a backdrop within a theater production itself. [35] Presumably these painted illusions were installed at the time the gardens were built in the 1630s, before *Miramé* was staged.

Following along the garden walks at Rueil on his way to the cascade, Evelyn had passed by the *Citronierre* and its parterre, where the boxed orange trees were set out in rows during the summer. Forming one side of the parterre and at a right angle to the orangery stood what appeared to be a dramatic, full-scale model of the Roman Arch of Constantine in Cardinal Richelieu's garden (Fig. 65). In fact, the magnificent triumphal architecture was a piece of theater art "painted on a wall in oyle, as large as the one in Rome," Evelyn recorded with astonishment. It was so well done "that even a man skilled in painting may mistake it for stone and sculpture."[36] The perspective seen through the arch, in fine disregard for its actual setting against a flat garden wall and surrounded by trees, framed a distant Italianate view of sky and mountains. The real orange trees, immaculately fake in their manicured appearance and carefully placed before the painted arch in cases, further complicated the theatrical imagery of nature imitating artificial trees.

Later in Paris, Evelyn also visited the interesting town garden of the Hôtel de Liancourt. The hôtel had been remodeled in 1623 by Richelieu's architect, Lemercier, who had also designed Rueil. Outside of his study and bedchamber, the Comte de Liancourt had installed a private garden in a small, narrow space that had been enlarged by means of a painted perspective placed against the enclosing wall. A stream of water ran through the garden and appeared to Evelyn "to flow for some miles by being artificially contained in the painting, when it sinkes down at the wall." It was, Evelyn admitted, " a very agreeable deceipt."[37] At the other end of the little space, the count had also built a miniature theater with "figures of

Veuë de l'Orengerie et de la Perspective de Ruel.

men and women paynted on light boards, and cut out, and by a person who stands beneath, made to act as if they were speaking, by guiding them, and reciting words in different tones as the parts required."

Full-scale garden theaters and spaces for entertainments were not new and had earlier appeared in Italian Renaissance gardens of the Villas Mondregore and Borghese. In a plan for a Medici palace in the Piazza Navona in Rome, Giuliano da Sangallo made a theater one of the principal defining elements of the garden design.[38] The garden had also penetrated the theater, and the convention of the garden scene in Italian and later in French drama was universal by the seventeenth century. The garden locale had first entered the theater through the court masques, pageants, and ballets. In the absence of permanent theaters, temporary ones were set up in the garden, or the garden itself was used as an open stage, where the natural backdrop was incorporated into the decor of the spectacle, as we have seen in the water carnivals at Fontainebleau. In the famous *Le Ballet Comique de la Reine Louise,* an elaborate dance drama staged in 1581 by the court, the King was flanked by the arbor of Pan and a grotto decorated with illuminated trees. The main action was centered on the garden of Circe at the opposite end of the hall. Satyrs, nymphs, pastoral virgins, and other garden denizens swelled the throng of dancers and chorus celebrating Elysian pleasures.

While permanent garden theaters did not appear in France until later in the seventeenth century when Le Nôtre included an open air theater in his new plans for the Tuileries, (Fig. 66), the garden continued to be a popular place to stage pageants and to perform pastoral plays and masques. The classic garden background—reversing the idea of using a painted perspective to enlarge a real garden—was a perfect setting for popular rustic dramas, as well as for court rituals (Fig. 67). In the Spanish gardens of Bueno Retiro, a theater had been built by Philip IV in 1637. The back of the Spanish stage could be removed and opened up to show the park beyond whenever the dramatic action called for a view of a natural landscape or garden scene.

At Versailles, Le Nôtre's *allées* and walks exploited techniques of perspective on a majestic scale and modified the earlier fixed perspective of the theater set by introducing a number of dynamic focal points with converging and intersecting avenues. The open-air fêtes and theater productions with magnificent illuminations and fireworks would actually take advantage of the perspective of the radiating walks, incorporating them into the staging (Fig. 68). In the engravings of the *Plaisirs de l'Île Enchantée,* the great spectacle of 1664, we see the garden avenues incorporated into the temporary setting in order to create a theatrical perspective

Le Theatre planté
de Piscias, Iss, et Maroniers
d'Inde

Parterre

La Salle de La
Comedie

degrez   Buis.
de Pierre reuestus

Amphitheatre

Tuileries   66

BALLET
DE LA JEUNESSE

T. Berin In.   Dolnar F.

Ballet setting   67
ft. Latona @ Versailles

Seconde Journée
Theatre fait dans la mesme allée, sur lequel la Comedie, et le Ballet
de la Princesse d'Elide furent representeé.

Versailles Backdrop   68

for the tableaux (Fig. 69). The view of the Banquet on the first day of the fête shows the diners, like actors, placed in a great amphitheater and set within a stage perspective formed by the trees, as the servants produced the food in the choreographed ritual of a *corps de ballet* (Fig. 70). A third engraving shows the setting of the Enchanted Palace on the *Île d'Alcine,* which was actually built in a water basin, where two giant stage wings were placed to accelerate the focus of the perspective centering on the Palace itself (Fig. 71). The entire garden had become a part of the theatrical experience through the unrestricted use of both natural and artificial perspectives that exploited the almost limitless possibilities of the surrounding space.

The King himself, who had regularly appeared in theatrical court productions as a young man, took a personal hand in utilizing to the fullest all of the architectural and natural features of his new park for spectacles and theater. In 1674, the *Grotte de Thétis* was used as a kind of permanent court theater set, becoming the setting for a production of Molière's *Le Malade Imaginaire* (Fig. 72). The three gates were thrown open so that the Perrault's façade, instead of being a mere background, became a stage screen through which the scenes performed in the well-lit interior were visible, transforming the stone of the architecture into the insubstantial form of a painted canvas backdrop. The façade of the *Grotte* resembled in many details Palladio's Teatro Olimpico at Vincenza, and the three arched openings recalled the triumphal arches of ancient Rome used so widely in the sixteenth and seventeenth centuries to evoke the King's connection with Roman glory. In the fêtes of 1668 a temporary arch was placed at the head of the garden *allées* at Versailles, transforming the lines of the walks into a natural perspective running through the arch that was at once a stage proscenium and a triumphal gate into the park.

By the time André Mollet published his *Jardin de Plaisir* in 1651, a growing sense of space on a monumental scale was becoming an essential part of the theory of French garden. Where, a century before, Éstienne and Liebault's *La Maison Rustique* had been directed toward the modest aspirations of the bourgeois

Marche du Roy, et de ses chevaliers, auec toutes
leurs suittes, au tour du Camp de la course de
Premiere Journée
bague, représentant Roger, et les au tres Chevaliers
enchantez, dans l'Isle d'Alcine

Premiere Festin du Roy, et des Reynes, auec plusieurs Princesses et Dames, seruy de tous les mets et presens faits par les Dieux et les quatre saisons. *Journée*

70

Troisiesme Theatre dressé au milieu du grand Estang representant l'Isle d'Alcine, ou paroissoit son Palais enchanté, portant d'vn petit Rocher dans lequel fut dancé vn Ballet de plusieurs espritz, et apres quoy ce Palais fut consumé par vn feu d'artifice representant la rupture de l'enchantement apres la fuite de Roger. *Journée*

71

Troisième Journée.
Le Malade imaginaire, Comedie representée
dans le Jardin de Versailles devant la Grotte.

Dies tertius.
De Ægrinoson, seu Æger imaginarius, Comædia acta
in hortis Versaliarum ad fores Cryptæ.

72   FAcAde Grotte of VersAilles

gardener, Mollet opened with the plans for a model pleasure garden, which, in fact, turned out to be nothing less than the Tuileries garden. Throughout the seventeenth century one can see the garden's edges opening out, claiming more and more of surrounding nature as a part of its stage setting. As the garden finally extended toward the furthest horizon, making the sky itself a part of the garden theater under Le Nôtre's stagecraft, one can see the role that the science of "the purest lights of the *optiques* and the most regular perspectives" had begun to play in landscape design. The manipulation of the length and width of *allées* and walks, the use of large sheets of water with its optical distortions, and even the painted garden "perspectives," a technique Mollet also recommended, demonstrated the creative influence of the theater upon the art of the garden as the two art forms intersected.[39] At Tanlay the canal leading to the classical grotto, itself a piece of theatrical design, was actually narrowed in order to increase the perspective illusion of great length (Fig. 73).

As we shall see, the theater continued to be an important influence on the French garden until the end of the eighteenth century. In 1780, the architect, Le Camus de Mezières, recommended to garden designers that theatrical effects be used in garden composition. "Let us turn your eyes to our Theatres," he wrote in *Génie de l'architecture,* "where the simple imitation of nature determines our affections. Here is the enchanted Palace of Armida; all is magnificent and voluptuous; one believes that love built it. The scene changes; it is the dwelling of Pluto that brings terror to our souls. Do we see the Temple of the Sun? It produces admiration. The sight of a prison causes sadness. Apartments arranged for a festival, surrounded by gardens with fountains and flowers, make us happy and prepare us for pleasure."[40] It was advice that reflected an old tradition in the gardens of France (Fig. 74).

Prosp. du Parc. et du Canal de Tanlai

Caig.

La Grotte.

TANLAY

73

La Conqueste de la Toison d'or Par les Argonautes

74

Fig. 63—*Homme en habit be Ballet.* Jean le Pautre illustrated a number of ballet costumes in garden settings. (Cabinet des Estampes, Bibliothèque Nationale)

Fig. 64—Schematic view of Cortile del Belvedere. The ideal viewpoint as seen in this drawing from the papal apartments looked onto the intermediate court as a stage. A variety of court entertainments were carried out in the courtyard below. (Photograph courtesy of Arnaldo Bruschi and published by Thames and Hudson in *Bramante,* 1977)

Fig. 65—*Rueil.* Triumphal arch is painted in *trompe l'oeil.* (Collection of the author)

Fig. 66—*Tuileries.* Garden theater designed by Le Nôtre. (Dumbarton Oaks Garden Library)

Fig. 67—*Ballet de la Jeunesse.* The garden setting for the ballet uses the Fountain of Latona and the palace of Versailles as its natural backdrop. (Cabinet des Estampes, Bibliothèque Nationale)

Fig. 68—*Plaisirs de l'Île Enchantée.* The interior of the theater has been constructed out of trees and hedges to frame the stage looking into the actual garden at Versailles. (The Metropolitan Museum of Art)

Fig. 69—*Plaisirs de l'Île Enchantée.* The palace can be seen through the central perspective. The trees of the garden have been incorporated into the set. (The Metropolitan Museum of Art)

Fig. 70—*Plaisirs de l'Île Enchantée.* The perspective has been closed for this sequence. (The Metropolitan Museum of Art)

Fig. 71—*Plaisirs de l'Isle Enchantée.* The orchestra is seated beneath the stage flats placed at the sides of the basin. The destruction of the palace with fireworks climaxed the fête. (The Metropolitan Museum of Art)

Fig. 72—The façade of the *Grotte* at Versailles transformed into a stage set. (The Metropolitan Museum of Art)

Fig. 73—*Tanlay.* The forced perspective of the canal in front of the grotto increased its theatricality. (Bibliothèque Nationale)

Fig. 74—Garden fireworks. The use of fireworks in gardens extends back into the sixteenth century and became a major feature of the garden tableaux staged at Versailles in the seventeenth century. See P. Bracco, *Fire Works-feux d'artifices.* Catalogue, National Gallery of Art, Washington, 1976.

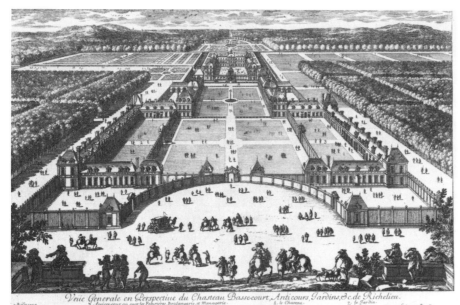

Veüe Generale en Perspective du Chasteau, Basse-court, Anti cours, Jardins, &c. de Richelieu.

Richelieu

75

Flore et Perspective de la Demie Lieu qui est au bout du grand Parterre.

II

76

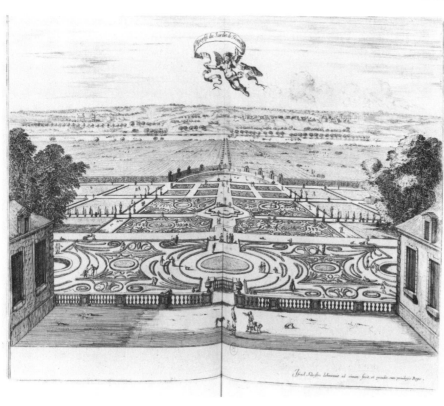

FreMONT

77

IV. Labors In Perfection

1. Le Nôtre

Between André Le Nôtre's birth in 1613 at his father's house on the edge of the Tuileries gardens, and his death in 1700, the classic French garden was to assume its decisive form. It should be clear by now, however, that the dynamic shape that the garden took under Le Nôtre's direction, and through the patronage of Louis XIV, was the result of a long tradition. It was the result of an evolution which had gradually elevated the work of the garden designer into that of a major art form capable of serving the highest policies of the state, and sharing in importance with architecture, painting, and sculpture.

The deliberate, luxurious nature of garden art on a grand scale not only required great quantities of money and social stability to enable uninterrupted physical growth, it also required the cultivation for generations of the traditional skills of gardener-architects such as the Le Nôtres and Mollets. The passionate devotion to gardening of successive French kings was to provide these necessary foundations for the unparalleled achievements in garden art during the reign of Louis XIV.

Even though, in theory and in practice, French garden art emphasized the formal subordination of nature to reason and order, there was, in fact, a widespread, almost romantic awareness of nature expressed by Le Nôtre's contemporaries. Poets, novelists, nobles, and bourgeoisie conveyed a deeply felt and coherent appreciation of nature's pleasures. The daily walks through the royal parks noted by Evelyn, the frequent country outings recorded in letters and diaries, the ritual of the royal hunt, the growing curiosity reflected in scientific studies of nature's mysteries and, above all, the cultivation of the garden itself, is evidence of a pervasive awareness of nature's beauty and delight. One has only to glance at Jean Gombust's famous map of Paris and its environs published in 1652 to see how extensive gardening had become, spreading from the royal parterres of the Luxembourg and the Tuileries to the private gardens in the Marais. "The culture of gardens has at all times been considered the first art of the world," the author of *Le Jardinier Solitare* declared in his introduction. "It is the pleasure I commend to a man of enquiring mind, who shaking off the noisy life of the world . . . chose to pass the remainder of his days in his country house, in order to taste the happiness of a life of innocence that one finds in rustic life."[1]

The Le Nôtre family was one of a half dozen families of gardeners who, by the late sixteenth century, controlled most of the royal gardening positions. Le Nôtre's father, Jean, had inherited his post as superintendent of six of the great parterres of the Tuileries from *his* father, Pierre, who had also worked in the gardens as early as 1572. Jean Le Nôtre's career at the Tuileries had progressed under the supervision of Claude Mollet, who directed the work on the garden before he wrote his *Théâtre des plans et jardinage* in the 1590s.[2] It is significant that the treatises of the

Mollets and that of Jacques Boyceau were based on actual gardening experience, reflecting long-established taste and ancient skills which were also a part of André Le Nôtre's background and family training.

Following Jacques Boyceau's recommendations for professional training in landscape art as outlined in his *Traité,* the young Le Nôtre studied mathematics, geometry, architecture, and also painting — for at one point he had apparently considered becoming a painter. The studio of Simon Vouet, the painter-in-chief to Louis XIII, was selected, and there he was to meet a fellow student and future powerful colleague, Charles Le Brun. Vouet's studio introduced Le Nôtre to a stimulating collection of drawings and sketches made by Vouet during his extensive travels in Italy and the Near East. Vouet's drawings of Turkish gardens and arabesque designs were as much a part of Le Nôtre's studies as were the folios of Italian engravings of paintings and architecture the painter had also collected. It may well have been this early experience that later inspired Le Nôtre to become an art collector. Paintings by Poussin and Claude, and sculpture by Michelangelo and Michal Anguier were among the gifts from his collection that Le Nôtre gave to the King in his old age, for throughout his life Le Nôtre had been well paid for his services to the King.

During the early years of Le Nôtre's studies and professional training, garden design and practice was entering a new phase of development, due in no small part to the building boom of gardens and parks in and around Paris in the 1630s and 1640s led by the example of Cardinal Richelieu. With a megalomania that seemed to hound Richelieu through most of his life, at about the time as he was having the Sorbonne and the Palais Cardinal rebuilt (1627–1637), he also commissioned his favorite architect Jacques Lemercier to begin a new château and town, to bear the Cardinal's name (Fig. 75). The scale of the Château de Richelieu and its planned environs on a flat topography is astounding, anticipating the development at Versailles thirty years later. Even La Grande Mademoiselle was impressed, though not surprised, by the Cardinal's extravagance, "since it was the work of the most ambitious and ostentatious man in the world." Le Nôtre was familiar with Lemercier's work for the Cardinal at Rueil, where he may have worked as a young man, and it is probable that he also worked on the Richelieu gardens.

The approach to Richelieu's new palace-town complex was via three roads laid out in the pattern of the *"patte d'oie"* converging on a circle three hundred feet in diameter.[3] After passing through a series of large courtyards, the château, standing on a terrace platform, was entered by passing across a bridge over a moat. On the garden side, a fountain centered in another moated parterre directed the eye to a large, subtly tilted half-circled space built into an enclosing wall that was reminiscent of Boyceau's Luxembourg plan (Fig. 76). At the Château de Fremont, where the gardens were laid out at about the same time, the exedra, following closely the design at Richelieu, formed a water basin within the large half-circle and was fed by ten low fountains placed around the edge (Fig. 77). John Evelyn was so impressed by the layout at Fremont that he included it along with Richelieu in a list of French gardens drawn up in 1657 as a guide for a projected book on the history of the garden.

Two canals formed, as at Vaux, from an existing river and on a line with the moat on either side of Richelieu, carried the perspective through the cross axes of the great open park that was, in fact, as long as the central avenue from the entrance. Richelieu clearly expressed the classic garden system of the *"jardin de l'inteligence,"* and the garden structure of Versailles was prefigured as an abstract representation of the cosmos (Fig. 78). First, the château was placed in a central position of importance to the composition and to the perspectives. Secondly, the scheme was composed according to the main axis, a rule that was especially adhered to by all the leading practitioners, including Le Nôtre, Le Vau, and Hardouin-Mansart. A third principle followed at Richelieu was that the terrain

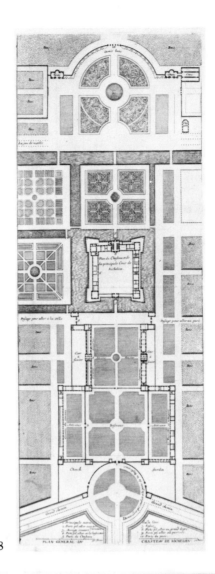

Riche lieu

78

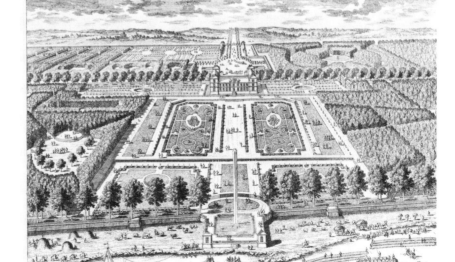

Petit-Bourg

79

LE CHASTEAU DE PETIT BOURG appartenant à Mr le Duc d'Antin au quel il doit la plus grande partie de ses embelissemens est une des plus belles maisons de plaisance qu'il y ait aux environs de Paris sa situation avantageuse sur un terrein en pente qui se termine au bord de la Seine fait pour d'un bon air et d'un...

had to be adapted to the discipline and structure of the composition. The measurable relationship of the architectural elements of Lemercier's composition at Richelieu, the use of water to relieve the monotony of the flat ground, and the placing of the parterres as well as of the château on a series of monumental, floating platforms, translated the basic principles of the formal garden into a powerful Cartesian grid where art and nature were bound together by mathematical regularity. The simplification of the vast, open spaces allowed no secrets, but only an idealized existence enforced by an inexorable logic.

Before entering the major phase of Le Nôtre's career, with Vaux-le-Vicomte, the garden at Petit-Bourg, although largely ignored by historians, adds another dimension to the picture of the rapidly evolving style which Le Nôtre carried to its limit during the later half of the century. The Château de Petit-Bourg and its garden was designed by François Mansart for the Abbé de la Rivere on the side of a gentle hill above the Seine, and was completed in 1655. A recent study of Mansart's works suggests that young Le Nôtre may have actually participated in the development of the design of the garden (Fig. 79).[4]

The sloping terrain of Petit-Bourg enabled Mansart to use moving water to establish the central axis by creating a cascade between the two great parterres of the dramatic fountain. The jet, sending a stream of water fifty or sixty feet into the air, was centered upon the château on the hill above and rose from a basin built into a rectangular earthwork projecting outward from the base line of the garden to the edge of the river. From the upper terrace of the house the fountain would have appeared to have shot up from the river itself. The main avenue leading from the château was extended beyond the far horizon into infinity by double rows of trees that unified the composition, stretching from the river to the sky. The Duc de Saint-Simon recounts the story that when Louis XIV criticized the position of the main *allée* that blocked the view from the royal bedroom, the offending trees were silently removed during the night without waking the visitor.

80 Versailles

2. Versailles

The first gardens at Versailles were too modest to attract much attention or comment from contemporary travelers and diarists. In an age when everyone who could manage it was building a new establishment and, more often than not, using funds taken from state coffers, Louis XIII was notably restrained. Richelieu and Mazarin spent millions of public funds on their palaces and retreats. The banker De Longueil could easily afford all of Mansart's costly changes to create the masterpiece of *Maisons*. During the first fifty years of the seventeenth century it is estimated that, in Paris alone, more than three hundred new *hôtels* and gardens were built.[5]

In 1627, a few years before Louis XIII ordered the old hunting lodge at Versailles rebuilt, the Maréchal de Bassompierre noted in his memoirs that the King was "not carried to building" at the expense of the country, "unless one wishes to reproach him for the lowly Château de Versailles, in whose construction even a simple gentleman could not take pride."

Jacques Menours, who had succeeded to the title of *intendant général des jardins du roi* when his uncle, Jacques Boyceau, retired, may well have asked his uncle and mentor to collaborate with him in laying out the grounds of Louis's hunting lodge. The overall structure of the first garden plans for the "little paste-board château" that stood on the edge of an unpromising forest and marsh was simplicity itself, reflecting a dogged clarity and order. In the central axis running through the middle of the château—a line Le Nôtre would maintain and extend to the horizon years later—one sees the continuation of a tradition that began in the gardens of Ancy-le-Franc and Charleval. "The abstract symbol of the world," as Paul Shepard observed in *Man in the Landscape*, "became in a sense the world itself."

The design for the large parterre in front of the château was illustrated by Boyceau in his *Traité* (Fig. 80) and extended the full width of the building of approximately 175 feet. The central avenue continued through a length of woodland, ending at an elongated quatrefoil-shaped basin similar to the one seen in the plan of Richelieu. The size of the three fountains placed along the axis were successively increased and the *allée* deliberately widened in stages as it ran to the terminal point, providing a subtle optical play with perspective and foreshortening. Lemercier used the same, though less pronounced, technique at Richelieu, and it was no doubt used in other gardens of the period (Fig. 81).

It was this modest beginning at Versailles that Louis XIII's son inherited and would transform from a few acres into the most extravagant and influential garden in European history. By the time he began to work on "that most dismal and thankless spot . . . *sans bois, sans terre, sans eau,*" in the words of the Duc de Saint-Simon, Le Nôtre was already a mature, professional garden designer with twenty-five years of experience.

Le Nôtre's name, after he became famous as the King's chief gardener and one of the three *surintendants des bâtiments,* has been generously associated in retrospect with any number of garden projects during the 1640s and 1650s, but actual details of his work or development before Versailles are sadly lacking. The gardens of Maisons, Wideville, Richelieu, Petit-Bourg, Rueil, and Fremont have all been mentioned as being a part of his early experience. But the list could be doubled without adding much to our understanding, in the absence of drawings and documents to show us exactly the sources of his ideas or the methods he used to achieve the desired results.

Among the powerful and newly rich patrons of the arts during the creative, volatile period of Louis XIV's Regency, patrons who took freely from the state to carry out their aggrandizing building schemes, was Mazarin's treasurer, Nicolas

 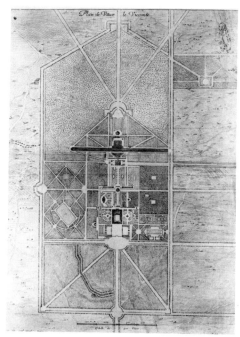

"du Bus" plan for Versailles ⁸¹   Vaux-le-Vicomte ⁸²

Fouquet. With an extraordinary ability to attract artists to his circle — painters, sculptors, composers, poets, and architects — Fouquet was one of the most influential cultural forces at that brilliant moment. Anatole France said that he nurtured artists with a "noble delicacy." Given the range of Fouquet's prodigal interests and taste, it is not surprising to find gardening among them.

In 1652, six years before Fouquet had asked Le Nôtre to join his friend Charles Le Brun and the architect Louis Le Vau to work as a team on the new Château at Vaux-le-Vicomte near Melun, Charles de Sercy, the publisher of Claude Mollet's *Théâtre des plans et jardinages,* dedicated the volume to Fouquet. In the dedication, de Sercy praises the *"superbes jardins de Vaux-le-Vicomte,"* suggesting that the basic lines of the garden at Vaux had already been established before Le Nôtre took over their direction in 1657.[7] The practice was to lay out the general structure of the grounds at the time the foundations for the building were begun so that the trees and plants would be mature when the château was completed. This may well have been the case at Vaux.

The essential element to grasp about Vaux or Versailles or Chantilly or any of the other great classic French gardens is that they were not the creation of one artist's vision or execution, but instead were the result of a complex and carefully tuned, collective effort by many talented men brought together to transform and shape nature into an acceptable work of art. The creation of a great garden in the seventeenth century was rather like the organization of contemporary pro-ductions of the new Italian opera or the French *Ballet de Cour;* a group of artists drawing together ideas that had been around, or in the air, for a hundred years. At Vaux, aside from the "Trinity" of artists who were to be apotheosized later for their work at Versailles, there was the *fontaineer* Claude Robillard, who made water as important a feature of garden art as the trees and marble; Villedo, the stonemason who built the grotto and canal; and Antoine Trumel, the chief gardener who supervised the actual labor of selecting, moving, and setting the plant material.

Sculpture, which had become such an important element in the garden, had to be commissioned, and its placement required special skill, as one can see in the superbly placed statues at the intersections of the walks at Fremont. Fouquet

VAUXE -le-
Vicomte

83

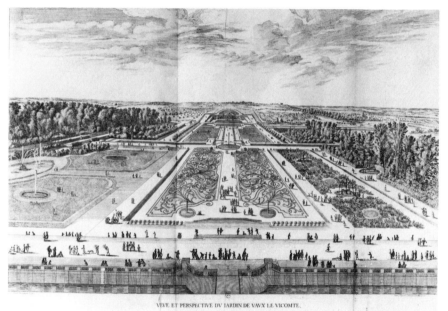

VEVE ET PERSPECTIVE DV IARDIN DE VAVX LE VICOMTE.

//

84

/

85

prevailed upon his friend, Nicolas Poussin, in Rome to produce a group of ornamental terms for Vaux. Michel Anguier, Lespaynandel, and Thilbaut Poissant were also given commissions.[8]

The gardens at Vaux were the most complex ever undertaken in France before, and the organizing force and personality behind such a stupendous enterprise had to have been the Minister of Finance himself, who could personally direct an undertaking of imperial magnitude. First, three offending villages were leveled and the river Angueil marshalled into a canal over three thousand feet long. Earth was moved to form massive terraces, parterres, and ramps, followed by tree planting on an imposing scale. A hospital was especially built for the workmen in a nearby village. When the major work was completed in 1661, the results of Le Nôtre's informing genius and that of his colleagues had created nothing less than a masterpiece (Fig. 82).

One has to imagine the ineffable chemistry of water and light playing over an enormous outdoor stage set, arranged for an entertainment on a pagan theme, in order to animate the engraved views of Vaux (Fig. 83). Standing on the short terrace directly in the center of the garden façade of Le Vaux's château, the eye can suddenly lose its hold on reality, or at least there is a "willing suspension of disbelief." The first impression is that all has been revealed in a glance, and the element of distance has been suddenly reduced to a comprehensible, theatrical gesture. Hercules, resting after his labors on the distant hill above the grotto, may be ten inches high or a hundred feet tall (Fig. 84 and Fig. 85). The heavy foliage on either side of the central parterres keeps the outline solid and directs the eye precisely toward the limits of its range at the horizon. Keeping the center of the space toward the horizon free of statues and other distractions, except for Hercules, allows the observer to stand there and feel that he is the center of the composition perceivable in its entirety.

The massing of tall groves of trees along the edge of a formal plan as a means of transition into the surrounding countryside was a technique long used in Italian Renaissance gardens, this merging of the formal lines of the boundary giving an appearance of extent and freedom. Nor was it new to French gardens, as we have seen at Montceaux and Richelieu, although in Silvestre's engravings of Vaux (Fig. 86), Le Nôtre's masterful handling of the *bois de haute futaie* as a background to the architectural elements of fountains, stairs, and grotto is superbly demonstrated.

The incorporation of the adjoining forest into the composition had been recognized and described by several garden theorists as a useful structural element of a garden, and providing a shaded retreat of walks and rides for visitors. Félibien remarked how the King at Versailles liked "to seek the fresh air, where the thickness of the trees prevents the sun's rays from penetrating . . . "[9]

The groves and the *bosquets* also could suggest that touch of natural simplicity or Elysian sanctuary which Le Nôtre and other designers liked to incorporate into the garden as a contrast to the formal elements. The spirit was similar to the dramatic contrast of the aristocratic pose of an elegant cast of rustic shepherds and shepherdesses in a seventeenth-century pastoral masque like Molière's *Florimen*. And not only the rustic, but the exotic as well, was hidden within these walks. At Vaux, Mademoiselle de Scudery's sharp eye did not miss the pyramids *"à la Memphis"* carefully buried in a corner of the woods and set among irregular grounds—*"En un petit coin de terre assez irregulier"*—although, regrettably, we have no further details.

The element of fantasy and unreality of Vaux increases as one begins to explore the complexity of the plan which, at first, had appeared so simple and self-evident. Three important transaxial walks reveal themselves as one proceeds down the grand *allée* toward the canal screened from the house. Foreshortening of the perspective is achieved by increasing the distance between each of the longitudinal divisions formed by the cross walks (Fig. 87).

Not only is the canal hidden below the terrace, but the magnificent cascade is

86 VEVE ET PERSPECTIVE DE LA FONTAINE DE LA COVRONNE ET DV PARTERRE DE VAVX

87 VEVE ET PERSPECTIVE DES PETITES CASCADES DE VAVX

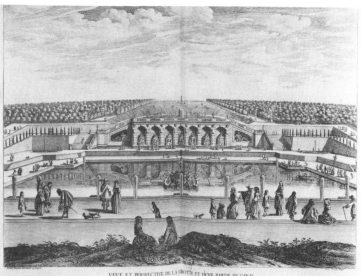

88 VEVE ET PERSPECTIVE DE LA GROTTE ET DVNE PARTIE DV CANAL.

also waiting there as well, facing the grotto on the opposite side of the water (Fig. 88). (Madame de Sévigné once stopped at Vaux to rest on her way to Paris "with the idea of bathing in the ornamental waters and partaking of two fresh eggs."[10]) Above the grotto the sloping ground has been scooped out, forming a steeply terraced hemicycle, providing yet another variation on this type of focal point we have already noted at the Luxembourg, Richelieu, and Fremont. The incline of the hill enabled Le Nôtre to give this amphitheater an upward tilt to distort the perspective. In the center of the hemicycle a single jet of water rose from a basin, reinforcing the vertical accent of the statue of Hercules placed on the axis further up the slope.

The strong central *allée*—running from the entrance of the château to the canal and continuing on a line with the fountain atop the grotto and on through the narrowing wall of trees to the horizon—celebrates the classical order and symmetry of the design. But it is only part of the deception that permeates the scheme. The smooth grass parterres on the left in front of the *Fontaine de la Couronne*, for example, are twice the size of the narrow compartments on the right, enameled by contrast with colorful flowers and plants (Fig. 89). Even though Le Nôtre seems to have had a prejudice against flowers in his compositions as being disturbing to the classical structure, extensive use of flowers throughout the seventeenth century was popular. Louis XIV was particularly addicted to extravagant plantings. Once, the entire color scheme of the gardens at Trianon was changed during the short span of the King's lunch, as if by magic. Madame de Maintenon complained of the heavy odor of tuberoses at Trianon, saying she had to remain inside to avoid it. In 1690, A. C. D'Aviler distinguished several types of parterres using flowers alone or in combination with boxwood accents.

The drop in the grade level on the left side of the *allée*, allowing Le Nôtre to sink the parterres and fountains below the terrace, subtly united the irregular levels of the ground at this point, which at first appeared flat to the eye, having been seduced by the main prospect (Fig. 90).

Fouquet's megalomania and self-deception, as reflected in Vaux's gardens, may well express that fatal hubris that led the financier to ignore the storm warnings, never suspecting that he was playing directly into the hands of Colbert, Mazarin's successor. The two famous fêtes Fouquet staged in the summer of 1661 for the court and the young King, celebrating Vaux's completion and precipitating his own downfall, have become a part of garden history, for they were seen as a prelude to the work Le Nôtre would carry out at Versailles after Fouquet's arrest.

Le Nôtre's creation at Vaux, aided by propagandists like La Fontaine and Mademoiselle de Scudery, brought him instant fame, and he received a number of commissions before he began to work on Louis XIII's old park at Versailles. It is difficult to date the actual beginning of his first phase, although it is apparent that plans were well under way by 1662. That winter twelve hundred trees arrived at Versailles from Vaux, following Fouquet's imprisonment.

As in almost every major garden on which Le Nôtre worked, he began at Versailles with an old scheme, staying at first within the walls constructed in the 1630s. The large basin at the foot of the central avenue was retained and remodeled, eventually becoming the *Bassin d'Apollon*. The longitudinal and transverse axes were also kept, while Boyceau's parterre was consolidated and supported by an artificial plateau and enormous circular earthwork now called the *rampe de Latone* (Fig. 91). In 1665, the same year as the *allée royale* was laid out, the principal lines of the *petit parc* had been established.

The sequence of the development of the gardens at Versailles is intimately related to the emerging power of the King, his concept of the monarchy, and his love affairs. All three influences were at times entangled in the expansion and use of the gardens to further the King's policies or to celebrate an amorous conquest. The growth of the King's power can be charted by the growing number of acres added to the gardens and parks, the annual increase in the daily water consump-

89

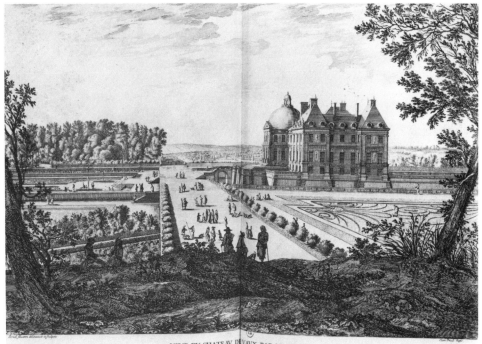

VEVE DV CHATEAV DE VAVX PAR LE COSTE

90

tion of each group of new fountains, or by measuring the length of the garden façade of the château itself each time Le Vau or Hardouin-Mansart extended it.

The spreading geometry of landscaped circles, squares, and intersecting walks—all centered on the main axis with several tranversal lines—provided the basic ordering devices which enabled Le Nôtre to maintain unity and continuity in the face of unpredictable expansion. By 1668, the year the King's power reached new heights with the triumphant signing of the treaty of Aix-la-Chapelle, the gardens had been stretched royally over hundreds of acres of ground. The ordering technique employed by Le Nôtre was additive and could be extended endlessly as the King's obsessions and growing power might require. The formula also allowed Le Nôtre to maintain a balance of proportion and scale between the architecture and the garden landscape itself, often anticipating later additions to the palace. There seems to have been a continuing element of madness in the megalomania at Versailles, and when the King finally tired of the whole business in his old age, he turned to the development of Marly and deliberately selected a site so rough and enclosed that he justified the new adventure in the hope that its rugged terrain would somehow contain his mania.

Versailles was not the kind of place where nothing could be added or taken away according to the classic formula, or where one could say even at a given moment that it had reached an equilibrium of perfection. In fact, many of the new spaces that Le Nôtre was constantly called upon to create were meant for only a single or particular function within the garden program. He understood the temporary, theatrical uses of the gardens in the endless variety of functions the King required of his disposable backdrop, especially during the early years of his reign before the court was moved permanently to Versailles in 1682 (Fig. 92).

Between 1663 and 1670, the functions of the gardens as *une grande folie*, theater, concert hall, botanical conservatory, and pleasure ground for distracting an increasingly jaded court whose real powers were being systematically removed, dictated the plans. Garden designing by the King himself became a royal occupation—in an ideal world of perfection where he stood at the center as chief architect, supreme over nature. The axis of the gardens and the avenues of Le Nôtre's new city, eventually reaching over eight miles in length, literally converged on the King's apartment (Fig. 93). As the image of his supremacy was gradually translated into stone and marble, *bosquets,* and fabulous water displays of unparalleled magnificence, the iconographic program inside and out, all relating to himself as *le roi soleil,* became more and more pervasive in its variations on that single theme (Fig. 94).

The *Grotte de Thétis* (Fig. 95), which was completed in 1664, and destroyed in 1684 to make way for Mansart's north wing, not only provides a good example of the singularity of Versailles, but it also demonstrates the complexity of symbolism that could be embodied within one architectural element in the garden. The examples could be multiplied from many of the major constructions, such as the *Bassin d' Apollon* and the *Fontaine de Latone.*

Designed by Charles Perrault and built in the corner of the main parterre to the north of the palace, the façade celebrated the legend of Apollo and Thétis in three bas-relief panels, and in the entrance gates. Mounted over the central gate was the gilded head of the Sun God himself, radiating beams which had been extended in the design of the ironworks onto the adjoining two gates. It was probably the first full-scale appearance of the Sun God theme in the decorations of Versailles.

Inside the temple-grotto, the story continued where the walls of Thétis's chambers beneath the sea were recreated in a fantasy of encrusted shell, shining mirrors, and rock work. In the center niche Apollo was "tended" by his adoring nymphs after his celestial labors of the day—and on each side, his faithful horses having pulled his chariot across the skies, were fed and watered (Fig. 96).[11] Fountains and jets played over the walls while a hydraulic organ hidden from

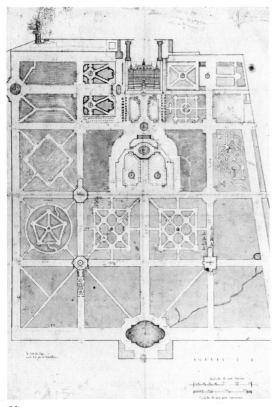

91

Versailles

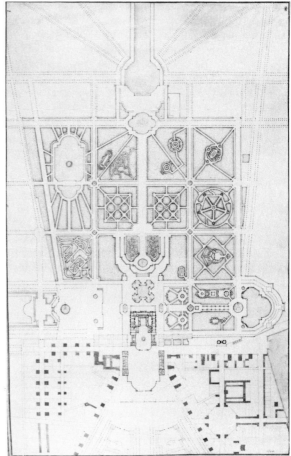

92

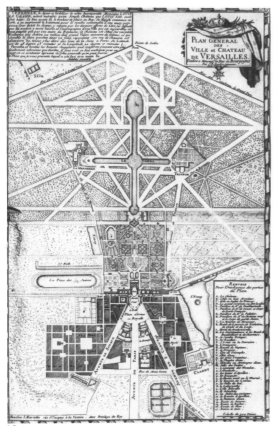

93

94

sight provided an acoustical illusion of singing birds, and shell-framed mirrors covering the walls multiplied the visual deceptions (Fig. 97).

The grotto was used by the King as a theater and banqueting hall. It also served as a water tower for a reservoir contained on the roof and seen in the reflected water in Patel's painting. Water pumped from the pond of Clagny below was held in a series of large reservoirs and was finally lifted even higher to the roof of the grotto in order to increase the pressure for the fountain jets below.

As at Hadrian's Villa at Tivoli, water was a ceaseless obsession at Versailles, a *Cité des Eaux*. It was given every conceivable shape and used in endless forms and combinations, from the great jet of the white column of water of the *obélisque d'eau* shooting eighty feet in the air, to the little garden called *La Source* at Trianon which Le Nôtre hid in a corner of the palace, with small artificial springs bubbling up and running off in contrived rivulets (Fig. 98).

The limited water sophistication of Louis XIII's original garden in the 1630s had required one rather primitive pump, but technical improvements in moving water had steadily progressed so that by 1664 a new water system with a horse-powered piston pump was installed, capable of delivering more than six hundred cubic meters of water a day. By the end of the first phase of the development of Versailles, in the summer of 1668, when the so-called Great Fête was presented in August, full-scale water displays were regular features of the garden entertainment, consuming more water in a day than the pumps of Samaritaine delivered to the entire population of Paris of 600,000 people.

But the continual expansion of the gardens constantly outran the existing water supplies. The total number of fountains at Versailles, Trianon, and Marly finally reached fourteen hundred. Vauban, the great military engineer, was consulted. Members of the Academy of Science were called in. Louvois, the Minister of War, undertook a disastrous scheme to bring the waters of the river Eure to the palace through forty miles of canals and aqueducts. The project was finally abandoned after ten years during which millions were spent and thousands of soldiers who had been pressed into the hopeless project died of injury and disease. In 1688, the machine of Marly, a wonder of hydraulic engineering of the time, was completed and fourteen water wheels lifted water from the Seine. Through a series of clanking pumps, channels, and aqueducts, it was carried to reservoirs more than five hundred feet above the river and could produce as much as five thousand cubic meters in twenty-four hours (Fig. 99).

With military victories abroad and the consolidation of all powers of state in his own hands, the King's ascendancy continued to be translated by Le Nôtre into new garden construction. In 1669, the extension of the canal to the west was begun as a continuation of the *allée royale* (Fig. 100 and Fig. 101). After the outer limit had been established by the lengthening of the canal to nearly a mile, and by the addition of the two arms enabling the far reaches of the park to be easily explored by boat, Le Nôtre turned to inventing ways of relieving the predictable monotony of the main outlines. In the groves between the lengthening axis, he introduced his famous *bosquets* and quincunx with their imaginative variations in the use of fountains and pools (Fig. 102, Fig. 103, Fig. 104, and Fig. 105).

Le Nôtre and other artists had observed during the various court spectacles staged at Versailles in the 1660s, that it made more sense to build a variety of more or less permanent garden apartments or rooms as theatrical settings for court functions rather than to continue the endless and wasteful construction of elaborate but perishable decorations. The *Théâtre d'Eau*, which was the *chef-d'oeuvre* of water engineering at Versailles, dates from this period, as does the labyrinth decorated with fountains and sculpture illustrating La Fontaine's *Fables*. Other major fountain groups included the Fountain of Latona (Fig. 106), dedicated to Apollo's mother, the Fountains of Four Seasons, and the magnificent Apollo group and fountain in the center of the *Bassin d' Apollon*. Le Nôtre, and the sculptors under the direction of Le Brun, had interpreted the iconographic pro-

Vue de la face exterieure de la Grotte de Versailles.   Exterioris Versaliana Cryptæ Prospectus

Le Grotte
de Versailles 95

Vue du fonds de la Grotte de Versailles orné de trois Groupes de Marbre blanc qui representent   Prospectus Cryptæ dinterioris Versaliana cohi fil inter Nymphas Thetidis,
le Soleil au milieu des Nymphes de Thetis et ses chevaux pansez par des Tritons.   et quæ equii cum Tritonibus statuæ marmoreæ celebrentur.

Interior
of Grotto 96

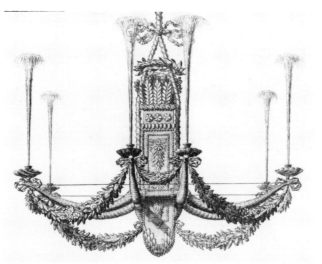

97

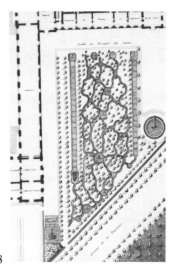

98

P.Martin
Versailles
99

100

102

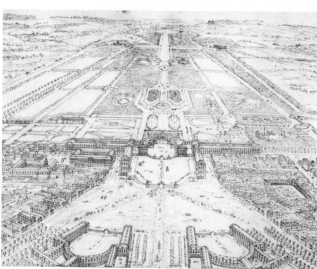

Versailles

101

Marais artificiel, entouré de Joncs d'airain, a de Jets d'eau. Palus artificialis iuncis aereis et aquis salientibus circumsepta.
Dans les Jardins de Versailles. In Hortis Versaliensis.

103

104

105

Latone entre les deux bassins Apollon et Diane, demandant vengeance à Jupiter
de l'insolence des Paisans de Lycie, qui sont changez en Grenouilles.

Latona, inter Apollinem solem et Dianam, Jovis maximi implorans
adventus Ægleas Rusticos, quos Deus reliae in : Ranas de format.

À Paris les Verilleu de Versailles
Chez Gallien ge Maty de Lembray.

Qu'illicet Rusticanos
Quod Trebbianus Maty Cuncticanos.

W.d Veyza Judy 1688

106

107

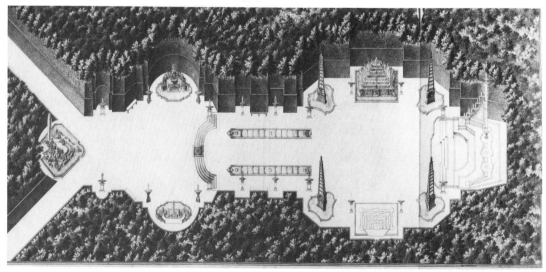

108

gram centered around Apollo, his family, and his court from every conceivable angle. As Félibien remarked concerning the cult of the Sun King: since the sun was the device of both Apollo and the King, "there is nothing in this superb mansion that does not relate to that divinity."[12] Other mythological themes were drawn from Cesare Ripa's great mythography translated into French in 1644, including the rivers of France appearing as ancient water gods, the four seasons, the four parts of the day, the continents, the four elements, and various gods of nature and mythology related to the garden.

Throughout all this stage of development, there is in Le Nôtre's designs a strong tendency toward an austere refinement with an architectonic strength welded into a coherence that contrasts sharply with the much more complicated and elaborate gardens created earlier in the century (Fig. 107). The brothers Francini, working first at Saint-Germain-en-Laye and later in a number of royal domains, had introduced and encouraged a more flamboyant Italianate use of fountains, cascades, grottos, and lattice works in less unified compositions. The movement toward greater simplification, both in composition and in the severely shaped and geometric elements, such as the palisades, the *allées,* and the background hedging, can be seen in Le Nôtre's late work (Fig. 108). Not only space, but time itself, as represented by the growing and ever-changing plant material, seemed to be fixed and held in suspension by the overwhelming authority of the King and his garden agents. Beneath the hard-edged, reductive perfection of ruthlessly shaped and controlled trees and bushes, one can sense an abstract, almost brutal love of power, which, of course, was the chief characteristic of the age.

The last phase of the work on the gardens at Versailles again followed policies of state, and coincided with the official establishment of Versailles as the official seat of government. In 1678, Jules Hardouin-Mansart received orders to enlarge the palace in order to accommodate the court and government. By 1689, the palace, as we now know it, was completed. To the north, Perrault's grotto was pulled down, and to the south, Mansart's great orangery, capable of holding more than two thousand trees, replaced Le Vau's smaller structure (Fig. 109). In order to follow the lines of the extension of the palace, a terrace was built and an artificial plateau carried to the edge of the orangery's roof where parterres set with boxed orange trees could be seen below. As the palace under Mansart took its final shape, the west terrace and parterre were completely rebuilt, finally achieving the present form of the two vast mirrors of the *Parterre d'Eau* as a solution to uniting

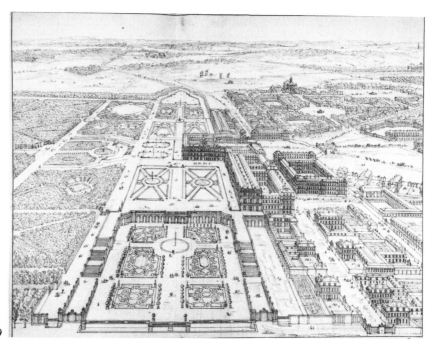

109

110

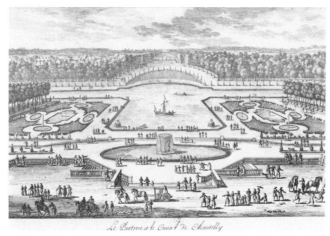

Le Parterre et le Canal de Chantilly

111

the architecture with the garden. A more perfect solution could not be imagined, yet the testing of various designs before the final one (proposed by the King himself) was executed, consumed nearly ten years of experimentation.

During the thirty years that Le Nôtre worked at Versailles, he also carried out a number of other commissions, but again, the detailed record is extremely limited. Even after his triumph at Vaux, before he had gone to Versailles, he had undertaken major alterations at Saint-Cloud as well as at Chantilly where, between 1660 and 1668, the great Condé had transformed the grounds of his old Renaissance castle.

First of all, the waterway of the river Nonette at Chantilly had been collected into a canal nearly as long as the one later built at Versailles. Since the moated castle was irregular in shape and not suitable as the centerpiece for a grand symmetrical scheme, Le Nôtre, in a brilliant move, placed the axis on a high terrace to one side of the château and extended it with the dramatic stone stairs (Fig. 110) that led down onto the terrace below and to the large water basin formed by the canal (Fig. 111). To prolong the axis, Le Nôtre extended the basin by enlarging the canal on the opposite side where the perspective of the view from the top of the great stairs looking across the canal was theatrically reinforced by heavy screens of elm trees. The vista was continued by an avenue running up the slope to the horizon above a steeply terraced hemicycle, strongly reminiscent of Vaux.

As chief of the royal gardens, Le Nôtre was, of course, requested to remodel other royal establishments, among them the gardens of the Tuileries, Fontaine-

112

113

bleau, Saint-Germain, and Trianon (Fig. 112 and Fig. 113). He completely re-worked the parterres and *bosquets* of Catherine de'Medici's old Paris garden of the Tuileries where she had established the original central avenue nearly a hundred years before. Even though Le Nôtre's inventive genius could not relieve that dull, flat site of its relentless monotony, he did create some individually beautiful garden rooms in the Tuileries, including one containing an open theater (Fig. 114). More importantly, he extended the central avenue to the horizon establishing the urban spine that would become the Avenue Champs Elysée.

Clagny and Trianon were among the few gardens of which the main plan can be fully attributed to Le Nôtre, since most of his work involved enlarging or remodeling existing schemes making it extremely difficult to identify specific details from his own hand. Although his unquestioned genius was his ability to control the subtle spatial balances over a vast area while obeying the prescribed rules of the formal garden, Le Nôtre's work was by no means limited to large official commissions on a royal scale. For example, the garden of Montmorency, Charles Le Brun's villa retreat near Saint Denis, shows Le Nôtre's daring skill in adapting the elements of the formal garden to a difficult, even eccentric and irregular topography of limited size.

A "Palace of Armide," the villa at Montmorency, looked out over a basin trapezoid in shape that distorted the perspective and heightened the theatrical illusion of an island when viewed from the narrow side across the still water (Fig. 115). The lines of the basin, when extended, converged on a fountain that stood at the apex and focal point of two walks running from the opposite direction and of

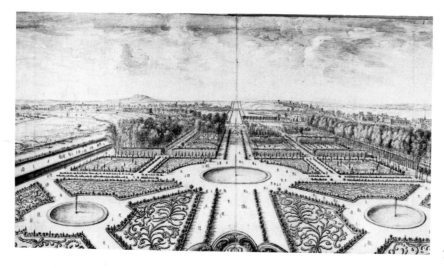

114

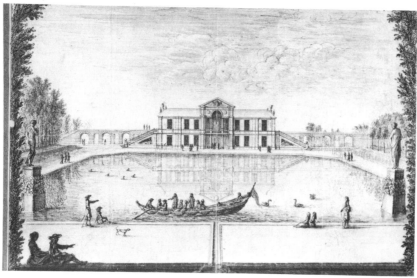

115

116

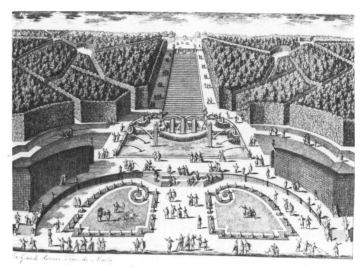

117   118

the same angle of degree as the basin itself.[13]

Beneath a high-rise apartment development in the suburbs of Paris, a few remaining walls mark the side of another Le Nôtre creation at the Château de Conflans (Fig. 116). When Le Nôtre was asked to rework the gardens of Conflans, both the château and the old layout presented a most chaotic challenge. Hamilton Hazelhurst has reconstructed Le Nôtre's renovations and again has demonstrated the master's ability to establish a harmonious composition over a difficult site.[14] "This garden is of a highly irregular form," Pignaniol de la Force later wrote, "but Le Nôtre knew how to cleverly correct the defects in the terrain." The *boulingrin* or sunken parterre surrounded by ramps and stairs and embellished with clipped plantings and wide surfaces of gravel around the octagonal basin with its single jet is unsurpassed in its noble equilibrium.

Although not designed by Le Nôtre, Marly, Louis XIV's hermitage located some five miles from Versailles, was hidden in a steep declivity surrounded on all sides by hills, and also presented a special challenge to its architect, Hardouin-Mansart, in his effort to accommodate the rules of the formal garden to topography even more unsympathetic than Le Brun's Montmorency. Taking advantage of the site that Saint-Simon labeled a "sewer of a valley," four great ornamental ponds, surrounded by terraces on which twelve small pavilions were placed before the royal pavilion, descended the length of the composition (Fig. 117). Behind the King's pavilion, a narrow cascade or water staircase, called the *rivière d'eau*, falling down the steep incline, completed the central axis (Fig. 118). The fall of the water was graduated so as to appear to be an uninterrupted stream when viewed at a distance. In the heavy woods on the slopes, a variety of *salles vertes* and *bosquets*, decorated with fountains and sculpture, were constantly built and rebuilt to relieve the boredom of the aging King and the small circle of courtiers who accompanied him there (Fig. 119 and Fig. 120). Saint-Simon said that within a period of six weeks, "fountains were altered a hundred times, and waterfalls redesigned in countless different ways. Goldfish ponds, decorated with guilding and delightful paintings, were scarcely finished," he went on, "before they were unmade and rebuilt . . . over and over again."[15] Marly narrowly avoided being dismantled during the Regency when the cascade was removed, but final destruction was carried out during the First Empire, although its skeleton still remains as a great public park of extraordinary beauty.

When Dr. Martin Lister saw Le Nôtre's mature gardens near the end of the century, he called them "labors in perfection." As a designer and, above all as a gardener, Le Nôtre was supreme in his work. If, as the *Mercure de France* said in his death notice in 1700, he had not thought that "fine gardens should resemble forests," neither did he believe they should be enslaved to repetitious, geometric forms.[16] With consummate skill, Le Nôtre had subjugated the visible landscape to the rules of his art. He had advanced the architectural lines of the Renaissance garden, which had been consciously evolved over two hundred years, to an ultimate form of spatial unity. The tranquility of order as reflected in the avenues, palisades, and *bosquets,* in the contrasts of light and shadow along the paths, the flashing fountains, and the tensions imparted by the sudden surprises or disintegrating vistas—all cast an irresistible spell over his creations. He had pushed visible space with a relentless clarity to the limits of perspective, reaching in his imagination beyond the eye itself to the extremes of logic on the far horizons of garden art.

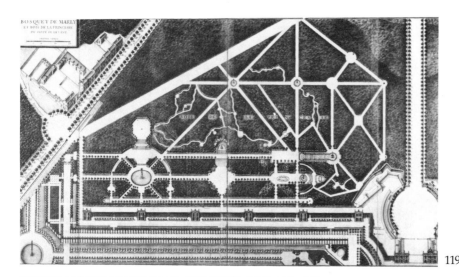

119

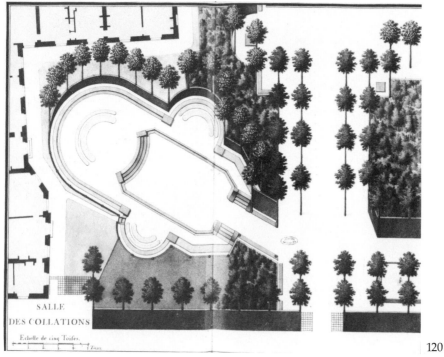

120

Fig. 75—*Richelieu.* (Dumbarton Oaks Garden Library)

Fig. 76—*Richelieu.* Jean Marot's view of the hemicycle which terminated the central axis. Sculpted parterres are similar to those of the Luxembourg. (Dumbarton Oaks Garden Library)

Fig. 77—*Fremont.* Aside from Silvestre's engravings, little is known of this beautiful garden. The placement of the statues at the intersection of the walks is exceptional and the sculpted

parterres *en broderie* are magnificent. (Bibliothèque Nationale)

Fig. 78—*Richelieu.* General plan. The converging roads on the entrance are similar to the later scheme at Versailles. (Dumbarton Oaks Garden Library)

Fig. 79—*Petit-Bourg.* A fountain formed parallel cascades on either side of the central walk in front of the château leading to the river. (Cabinet des Estampes, Bibliothèque Nationale)

Chapter IV (2)

Fig. 80—*Parterre du Château de Versailles.* Jacques Boyceau's spectacular embroidered parterres established his fame. The central round basin in his design for Versailles probably held a fountain. See Hazelhurst, *Boyceau.* (Cabinet des Estampes, Bibliothèque Nationale)

Fig. 81—*Versailles,* "du Bus" plan. Charles du Bus, who discovered this early plan of Versailles dated it between 1652 and 1661. Boyceau's central parterre (Fig. 80) can be seen in front of the château. The *potager* was located in the large square just to the left of the palace. The central axis later to be enlarged by Le Nôtre is already in place as the spinal cord of the composition. (Cabinet des Cartes, Bibliothèque Nationale)

Fig. 82—*Vaux-le-Vicomte.* Silvestre's engraved general plan dating from the 1670s is the earliest known. The canal that crosses the garden is one kilometer long. (Collection of the author)

Fig. 83—*Vaux-le-Vicomte.* Restored gardens viewed from central terrace of château. (Caisse Nationale des Monuments Historiques et des Sites)

Fig. 84—*Vaux-le-Vicomte.* Silvestre's view is approximately from the same point as Fig. 83. (Cabinet des Estampes, Bibliothèque Nationale)

Fig. 85—*Vaux-le-Vicomte.* The monumental copy of the Farnese Hercules was placed there in the nineteenth century. (Photograph courtesy of Roger Viollet, Paris)

Fig. 86—*Vaux-le-Vicomte.* Silvestre's view is looking across the width of the garden over the *Fontaine de la Couronne* immediately below the château, which is out of view to the right. The complex terraced levels are clearly shown. (Cabinet des Estampes, Bibliothèque Nationale)

Fig. 87—*Vaux-le-Vicomte.* The *petites cascades* were at the left end of the second cross walk below the château. (Cabinet des Estampes, Bibliothèque Nationale)

Fig. 88—*Vaux-le-Vicomte.* The original Hercules seen on the far horizon above the *grotte* was later removed to Sceaux by Colbert. (Cabinet des Estampes, Bibliothèque Nationale)

Fig. 89—*Vaux-le-Vicomte.* This parterre on an upper level was placed opposite the *Fontaine de la Couronne* (Fig. 86). It is a *parterre de fleur* and shows the rich use of flowers and plants within the formal green structure of seventeenth-century French gardens. Flowers on the scale required were, of course, a great luxury requiring trained gardeners, nurseries, and plant sources even in foreign countries. Louis XIV insisted on elaborate flower displays which became centered in the gardens of the Trianon. The numbers of potted flowers required for instant display numbered hundreds of thousands. No restored seventeenth-century garden today begins to approach this important and missing element of the formal garden. (Cabinet des Dessins, Musée du Louvre)

Fig. 90—*Vaux-le-Vicomte*. Silvestre's engraving as in Fig. 86 illustrates Le Nôtre's ingenious handling of grade levels. The *Fontaine de la Couronne* is out of view to the left. (Cabinet des Estampes, Bibliothèque Nationale)

Fig. 91—*Versailles*. This manuscript plan dating from 1677 showing the earliest garden scheme by Le Nôtre includes the famous labyrinth which can be seen at right center. It was later destroyed. A sketch for a fireworks piece is at the upper left-hand corner, while unexplained tents have been placed in the *allée* at the left below the fountain. (Cabinet des Estampes, Bibliothèque Nationale)

Fig. 92—*Versailles*. Silvestre's drawing of the *petit parc* dates from 1680. The rapid filling in of space with *bosquets,* water pieces, and walks can be seen by comparing with Fig. 91. (Cabinet des Dessins, Musée du Louvre)

Fig. 93—*Versailles*, 1693. The general plan of the gardens and park as fully realized at the end of the reign of Louis XIV. The gardening staff required to build and maintain Versailles and even lesser seventeenth century establishments was enormous. (Collection of the author)

Fig. 94—*Versailles*. The *Bassin d'Apollon* and the Grand Canal beyond. The miniature ships on the canal were used for mock naval battles. The sculpture group is by Jean-Baptiste Tuby. The original basin was created for Louis XIII in 1639 by Subet de Noyers but was altered later. (Cabinet des Dessins, Musée du Louvre)

Fig. 95—*La Grotte de Versailles*. In 1672 le Pautre engraved a number of views of the *grotte* before it was destroyed. A water reservoir was built into the roof behind the parapet. (Dumbarton Oaks Garden Library)

Fig. 96—Interior of the *Grotte*. (Dumbarton Oaks Garden Library)

Fig. 97—*Chandeliers de cocquillages et de rocailles*. (Dumbarton Oaks Garden Library)

Fig. 98—*Le Grand Trianon*. Le Nôtre's *bosquet* called *"La Source"* can be seen in the right corner of the wing of the château. The small, bubbling fountains and artfully meandering streams were a startling conceit in the middle of the formal structure. (Cabinet des Estampes, Bibliothèque Nationale)

Fig. 99—*Vue de la Machine et de l'Ague duc de Marly* by P. Martin; the painting is at Versailles. (Photograph courtesy of Lauros-Girardon)

Fig. 100 & Cover—*Bassin d'Apollon*. By P.D. Martin. The King in his wheelchair is making his promenade. (Photograph courtesy of Lauros-Girardon)

Fig. 101—*Versailles*. Silvestre's birds-eye drawing is viewed from the front of the palace looking over the canal to the horizon. The Trianon is to the right at the end of canal arm. The canal is 5,200 feet long and 400 feet wide. (Cabinet des Dessins, Musée du Louvre)

Fig. 102—*Le Bassin de la Sirene*. The fountain is the work of Gaspard et Balthazar Marsy. Le Pautre's engraving dates from 1679. (Dumbarton Oaks Garden Library)

Fig. 103—*Le Marais*. The design for the *bosquet* and fountain was inspired by the King's mistress, "la Montespan." Le Pautre engraved it in 1680. (Cabinet des Estampes, Bibliothèque Nationale)

Fig. 104—*Le Théâtre d'Eau*. The drawing showing the theatrical perspectives dates from 1700. (Cabinet des Dessins, Musée du Louvre)

Fig. 105—*Bosquet de la Salle de Bal*. Another of Le Nôtre's garden creations for court entertainments. (Cabinet des Dessins, Musée du Louvre)

Fig. 106—*Le Bassin de Latone*. Le Pautre's engraving dated 1678 shows the fountain before it was transformed by Jules Hardouin-Mansart. Latona was the mistress of Jupiter and the mother of Apollo. When Jupiter's wife Juno stirred up the peasants against his mistress, he avenged the insult by turning them into frogs. Two with metamorphosized head can be seen on either side of Latona. (Cabinet des Estampes, Bibliothèque Nationale)

Fig. 107—*Le Bassin de Bacchus*. This anonymous drawing dating from 1700 when compared to the more natural treatment of the *palissades* surrounding the fountain in Fig. 106 illustrates the gradual simplification which was taking place through the severe shaping of the plant material. The fountain group was painted in bright natural colors. Some of these have now been restored at Versailles. (Cabinet des Dessins, Musée du Louvre)

Fig. 108—*L'arc de Triomphe de Versailles*. The design for *bosquet* at Versailles, 1700, comes close to being a roofless pavilion with its walls and elaborate garden furniture and decorations. The floor or carpet was gravel. (Bibliothèque Nationale)

Fig. 109—*Versailles*. Silvestre's birds-eye view of Mansart's *orangerie* looking north across the *Parterre du Sud* and the *Parterre d'Eau*. (Cabinet des Dessins, Musée du Louvre)

Fig. 110—*Chantilly*. *La Fontaine de la Gerbe* is on axis with Le Nôtre's *Grand Escalier*. The old château can be seen at the left. (Dumbarton Oaks Garden Library)

Fig. 111—*Chantilly*. Birds-eye view looking from above the garden staircase across canal basin. (Cabinet des Estampes, Bibliothèque Nationale)

Fig. 112—*Meudon*. Le Nôtre's terrace and *allée* run from the new château (now destroyed) that was placed at right angles to the sixteenth century *grotte* on the side of the hill to the right, but out of view in Silvestre's drawing. The square basin flanked by orange trees was directly in front of the orangery built under the upper terrace of the château. (Cabinet des Dessins, Musée du Louvre)

Fig. 113—*Saint-Germain-en-Laye*. Le Nôtre's dramatic terrace running along the top of the hill above the river, which is to the right in the old photograph. (Photograph courtesy of Roger Viollet)

Fig. 114—*Tuileries*. Silvestre's drawing shows the gardens some ten years after Le Nôtre's remodeling in the 1660s. The *Arc de Triomphe* now stands on the far horizon. (Cabinet des Dessins, Musée du Louvre)

Fig. 115—*Montmorency*. Le Brun's Paladian villa and garden was near the village of Saint Denis, northwest of Paris. The grounds were greatly altered by Watteau's patron Pierre Crozat, who owned it in the eighteenth century. Rousseau was to know it later in that century. (Cabinet des Dessins, Musée du Louvre)

Fig. 116—*Le Château de Conflans*. A detail of Le Nôtre's garden from Martin's painting from around 1700. Nothing remains except portions of the stairs, upper right. (Photograph courtesy of Girardon)

Fig. 117—*Marly*. General plan. The water conduits from the reservoirs at the upper left can be traced. The King's pavilion at the base of the cascade was placed between the two hills. (Cabinet des Estampes, Bibliothèque Nationale)

Fig. 118—*La grande Rivière d'Eau de Marly*. The famous cascade in pink and green marble seen in Perelle's birds-eye view from above the King's pavilion. Some of the marble was used in the interior of Saint Sulpice when the cascade was destroyed. (Collection of the author)

Fig. 119—*Bosquet de Marly et Bois de la Princesse*. Placed on the steep slope, the *bosquet* seems to anticipate the winding, irregular garden layouts of the eighteenth century. (Archives Nationales)

Fig. 120—*Marly. Salle des collations*. The constant building and remodeling of Marly's *bosquets* and water pieces kept a bored King and his intimates preoccupied with an expensive playground. (Archives Nationales)

121

122

V. After Le Nôtre: A Sentimental Journey

"Such symmetry is not for solitude."

Lord Byron

In the 1787 edition of *Nouvelle Description des Environs de Paris,* J.A. Dulaure describes the country estate of the Comte d'Albon, a progressive aristocrat who had laid out a fashionable park near Franconville, not far from Paris. Its winding lanes and irregular sequence of organization declared the owner's taste for the latest garden layout with a "candour and truthfulness possessed by all honest souls . . ." In a grove where a statue representing "the first kiss of love, the tender, passionate scene so ardently described" in Rousseau's novel *La Nouvelle Héloise,* the Count paid homage to one of the decisive inspirations of the garden revolution. For it was Rousseau's discovery of nature, as everyone knows, that had compelled Frenchmen "to rise before noon," to look beyond their gilded drawing rooms into the surrounding landscape beyond their windows, and to walk in nature and solitude where previously they had, in the words of Taine, "only walked between tortured yews."

Further along d'Albon's walk was a classic temple dedicated to the Dying Christ where an altar held a relic of the True Cross, a medieval chalice, and the remains of a balloon which had made an abortive ascent toward heaven from the garden in 1784. On either side of the altar stood two statues dedicated to Love and Fidelity. Other features in the grounds included an obelisk fifty feet high, erected in honor of the Count's virtuous wife; an open-air room where white doves announced its dedication to friendship; a Lyceum Portico with busts of Montaigne and Rousseau; a lake adorned with statues of Seneca and Cato; a kitchen garden presided over by a statue of Priapus; monuments to Dutch and Swiss scientists; a devil's bridge with inscriptions from the *Roman de la Rose;* the tomb of a Protestant preacher whom the Count had befriended; pyramids in memory of two marshals of France, the Count's ancestors; a monument to the agricultural economist and Physiocrat, the Marquis de Mirabeau; a Swiss village where the Count actually lived with his wife and cows; a statue of Pan near the goathouse; monuments to William Tell and Benjamin Franklin; a mast of Liberty celebrating the Treaty of Peace in 1783; a cavern; and a medieval keep with "Gothic windows in the latest fashion" (Fig. 121).

In his eclectic Eden of emblems and conceits, d'Albon, "the virtuous and tenderhearted citizen, the friend of nature and mankind," managed to gather together the chief and often contradictory symbols of eighteenth-century culture. "Modernity and tradition, intellectual inquiry and emotionalism, religion and science, egalitarianism and aristocratic self-assertion, cosmopolitanism and patronism, artificiality and a yearning for naturalism" competed for a place in the Count's Elysium.[1] In fact, d'Albon's garden, where ideas grew like weeds, was only one rather eccentric manifestation of the garden revolution that had all but replaced the formal grandeur of the previous century.

By the end of the seventeenth century, the vision of the French formal garden, with its severe lines sweeping into infinity, had been fulfilled. The Renaissance ideal had reached its climax. Even before Le Nôtre had died in 1700, stagnation had set in, as the aging spectacle of the court pageantry and its tarnished garden sets, like a worn-out opera production, could no longer be convincingly renewed. Its star performer had danced his last ballet staged in the garden, and now in old age he was pushed onto the stage in a wheelchair in order to make his ritual promenade following the itinerary he himself had drawn up.[2]

Even if Le Nôtre's vistas had not reached their limits, or his endless variations in the *bosquets* and parterres had not revealed a certain exhaustion of imagination, the enormous cost of maintaining the grand style of Versailles and the other royal parks had strained the treasury nearly to the breaking point following the financial drain caused by the expense of the King's disastrous wars. As if to underline the chilling string of military defeats during the first decade of the new century, the bitter winter of 1709 caused further havoc. The hungry mobs of Paris actually rattled the gates of Versailles, and Saint-Simon's wine had turned to ice at dinner in his unheated apartment. Charlotte Elizabeth, the King's sister-in-law, reported that wolves were seen in the park at Marly where trees had been killed and gardens devastated by the freeze.

The growing bankruptcy of the government during the decade before the King's death in 1715 can be followed in the records of the declining expenditure on the royal gardens. For example, the annual cost of maintaining Marly's terraces and gardens was nearly 100,000 *livres* in 1698. By 1712 the yearly expenditures had fallen to less than 5,000.[3] What this meant to the precise, architectonic lines dictated by rules designed to control not only space but time as well, where trees were not to exceed a predetermined height by natural growth, can only be imagined. The Sun King's gardens, like his wars, were eventually reckoned in terms of the national debt. Liberated by the declining fortunes of the state, nature itself quickly reached out for a new freedom, enclosing avenues and filling in the open garden rooms of the Tuileries and the Luxembourg, embracing the classical statues, balustrades, and urns. Nature's metamorphosis transformed the old geometry into a poetically overgrown, seedy, Italianate landscape. It was an atmosphere of picturesque neglect familiar to all the French artists who had worked in the romantic, untidy gardens of Italy.

We see the transformation clearly in the drawings and paintings of Antoine Watteau (1684–1721), whose romantic eye and imagination were drawn to some of the more neglected parks around Paris when he arrived there in 1712 as a student from Valenciennes.[4] In Watteau's dreamlike landscapes the transformation of the "sad regularity" of the formal garden structure into a Claudian stage set, with full, towering trees now reaching to the sky and narrowing the once trim vistas, anticipated by a half a century the picturesque parks of Ermenonville and Méréville, where Hubert Robert's paintings both recorded and inspired the creation of those sylvan domains composed of similar romantic views. One of Watteau's favorite haunts during his first years in Paris was the garden that Le Nôtre had laid out for Charles Le Brun at Montmorency owned at that time by Watteau's patron Pierre Crozat, the rich merchant and art collector (Fig. 122). The garden's return to nature, masking the earlier artificial scheme beneath the voluptuous growth of the once trim and regulated trees, must have been calculated, for Crozat's great wealth precluded any thought of economic restraint. Watteau spent many hours in the peaceful surroundings of Montmorency, where years later Rousseau would discover the same "profound and delicious solitude." The paintings of Pater, Lancret, and Fragonard further document the dream-gardens of intimate picnics, music parties, and lovemaking played out within the old parks of the seventeenth century, now fashionably reduced and softened by an atmosphere of neglected untidiness that befitted the Regency's reaction to the formal grandeur of Versailles.

123

François Boucher who, more than any other artist typifies the spirit of the Rococo, collected Watteau's drawings as a young man. After his return to Paris from Rome in the 1730s Boucher joined the group of artists including Jean-Baptiste Oudry, Jacques-André Portail, and Charles-Joseph Natoire who frequented the ruined seventeenth-century park of the Prince de Guise at Arcueil near the Luxembourg's old aqueduct and made drawings there (Fig. 123). Through his friendship with Claude-Henri Watelet and his influence on the work of Hubert Robert, Boucher's connection with the French picturesque garden becomes apparent. Like many artists who contributed to garden designs, or who provided plans for garden structures, Boucher was also associated with the theater and worked with the *Comédie Française,* much as Watteau had earlier worked with the Italian theater in Paris.

The unfettered nature of Watteau's and Boucher's overgrown parks may have seemed to indicate a new, romantic taste reflecting a growing and visually articulate dissatisfaction with the past, but, in fact, the influence of Le Nôtre's formal school would still dominate the direction of garden design in France and throughout Europe for decades to come. Even before Le Nôtre had died, however, there were a few independent critics such as the Bishop of Avranches who saw no beauty in "the large broad sand-strewn *allées,* of trellises, parterres adorned only with a few delicate beds, defined by strips of box and edged with a few flowers and a few stunted trees, and in which you can scarcely distinguish summer from winter." For "although natural beauties are preferable to artistic," the Bishop continued, "that is not the taste of this century."[5]

If the French dreams of empire were in shambles at the end of the seventeenth century, the garden style of France ruled supreme throughout Europe, not only because of its adaptability, but also because it was easily taught and understood. In 1709 Antoine-Joseph Dezallier d'Argenville's (1679–1719) *La Theorie et la Pratique du Jardinage* appeared, becoming the standard work on the formal garden in successive editions and translations. Clearly and firmly, d'Argenville, assisted by Alexandre Le Blond (one of Le Nôtre's best students) in the third edition, laid out the elements of the style and the methods to achieve it, always beginning with paper, pencil, and ruler (Fig. 124). As in poetry and art, so in planning a garden, d'Argenville declared, nature must be consulted, which sounds very much like Rousseau's later advice to imitate nature. But to consult with nature was advice

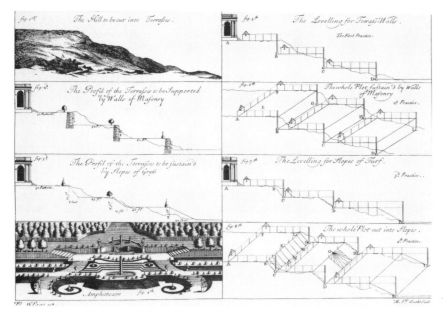

that ran through all of the early French garden treatises, even though the results, at least to our eye, were "eminently unnatural," in the words of Nikolaus Pevsner. This abstract notion did not mean that raw nature itself should be considered as a model for painters, poets, and garden designers, but rather that they should look to the vague, idealized notions of nature as distilled in the vanished gardens of ancient Greece and Rome and as seen through the imagination of contemporary Frenchmen. J. F. Félibien's reconstruction of the ancient Roman gardens of Pliny published in 1699 turned out, in fact, to be a perfect formal scheme for the *Grand Siècle.*

The other main points in d'Argenville's text and accompanying plans emphasized variety and simplicity within the formal structure. He warned against dividing and subdividing the space, an academic habit that had become so widespread that it threatened the very foundation of the spacious grandeur of Le Nôtre's late period. The extravagant shaping of trees into animals, charging knights, and green chessmen, was also criticized. Moreover, as if to anticipate the growing threat of English landscape gardens, readers were warned against adopting "the beautiful disorder of nature" without first correcting or amending her primitive state.

Even if the style of the formal garden could have been reduced to a cut and dried studio system and easily transplanted with reasonable success onto foreign soil as far away as St. Petersburg or Williamsburg, the art of Le Nôtre and his school had become too intimately tied to the political and social order of a conservative court to provide much incentive for creative activity after the epoch was over. Horace Walpole saw French gardens as "sumptuous and selfish solitudes . . . important displays of false taste," even though Philip Miller's influential *Gardener's Dictionary*, first published in London in 1724 and repeated in later editions, reinforced John James's translation of d'Argenville in perpetuating the formalist doctrine long after it had exhausted its creative drive. In 1765 the Chevalier de Jaucourt, in his article on *Jardin* for the *Encyclopédie*, continued to praise Le Nôtre's style as the model to follow.

Sir William Temple (1628–1699), whose words in *Gardens of Epicurus*, published in 1692, introduced a line of thought that was to revolutionize the gardens of England and the rest of the world in the eighteenth century, expressed his own taste for the formal gardens in his work at Moor Park. Although he might have preferred embroidered parterres and walled-in compartments of greenery, there were, however, "other forms wholly irregular, that may, for ought I know, have more beauty than any others . . . Something of this I have seen in some places, but heard more of it from others, who have lived much among the Chinese . . . where their greatest reach of imagination is employed in contriving figures, where the beauty shall be great, and strike the eyes, but without any order or disposition of parts . . ." The Earl of Shaftesbury's praise of the "horrid graces of the Wilderness" in 1709, to be followed shortly by the poetry and prose of Pope and Addison, further advanced a new doctrine of visual perception that would be as familiar in Paris as in London within a short time.

La belle nature had, of course, been celebrated by French writers in the seventeenth century. Madame de Sévigné seems to have enjoyed some of the simpler pleasures of nature and gardening when she wrote in the fall of 1671 that she had spent the morning at her country estate "in the dew up to my knees laying lines; I am making winding alleys all round my park . . ."[6] These few words anticipate by decades garden fashions that were to transform French gardening.

The first thing to note in Madame de Sévigné's letter is that here is a fashionable woman quietly enjoying herself in the solitude of the country when most ladies of her class would have preferred to be in the salons of Paris or Versailles. Secondly, she herself is actually working in the garden to lay out the walks—most surprisingly, the walks follow a "winding" pattern long before the Anglomania of curving, wriggling paths was to inundate the formal layout. Perhaps it was this special country pleasure described by Madame de Sévigné that the Abbé Pluche had in mind when he wrote *The Spectacle of Nature* in 1732, a book young Rousseau read and enjoyed. "Man in his innocence was from the earliest time destined to cultivate the earth, and we have not lost the feeling of our pristine nobility," the Abbé declared. "Any other occupation enslaves us or degrades us. As soon as we can be free and breathe a few moments at liberty, a hidden inclination brings us all back to gardening." If the Abbé had been English these lines would have been enshrined in the classic literature on the origins of the "Great Garden Revolution" in the name of liberty along with the words of Bacon, Milton, Temple, Shaftesbury, Kent, Pope, Addison, and the rest.

The revolution which was to overthrow the domination of the formal garden doctrine in the later half of the eighteenth century had its origin in England, although the ideas influencing the movement came from the previous century and from other countries as well as England.[7] English poets, philosophers, and novelists were widely read in France, and the same ideas that prepared men's minds for the changes to come in English gardens were freely circulated in French intellectual circles. Heroes and heroines of French novels, for example, began to appear in the country, far from Paris, where quiet walks and the contemplation of simple nature seemed to be their chief occupation. "As I walk I consider the works of nature and admire their variety. My efforts contribute to the birth and growth of some flowers and fruit which I have taken charge: I let my eyes wander over the peaceful landscape which surrounds me," Prevost wrote in *Memoirs d'un Homme de Qualité*.[8]

Given the fluid intellectual atmosphere in France at the end of the seventeenth century, and during the Regency following the death of Louis XIV, it is easy to see why literary writings of the English nature worshippers who called for gardens with individuality and variety were popular. In fact, Addison's praise of the natural, the various, and the unexpected in gardens was, as Pevsner has said, an unwitting application of the Rococo to landscape design instead of interior decoration, where the style had first appeared in France. The concept of variety and contrast in garden theory had been a part of the classic French treatises of the seventeenth century, although Boyceau or the Mollets were suggesting nothing remotely resembling a natural informality of the English variety. In the introduction to his treatise, it may be recalled, Boyceau referred to the elements of variety to be found in nature. Later in Book III he declared that "following the teachings Nature gives us in so much variety, we feel the most varied gardens are the most beautiful."[9] Boyceau also preferred the contrast and variety an irregular site provided, even though most gardeners of the day preferred the smooth, level layout that often led to dullness. At one point he even recommended a mixture of irregular, curved lines among the squares "so as to find the variety that Nature demands," but he hastened to add that curved elements were to be based upon the circle, the square, and the triangle, rather than nature's own deformities.[10]

Throughout Le Nôtre's career, he was often praised for his unexpected use of natural elements. "You know the manner of Le Nôtre," Madame de Sévigné wrote her friend Madame Grignan, concerning the new garden at Clagny in 1675, "he has left a little dark wood, which goes very well."[11] While the visual record is scant, Le Nôtre or others who worked under him at Fontainebleau must have allowed trees and plantings some freedom to follow nature, for Addison praised the carefully studied negligence of the gardens when he visited them. "The King has humoured the Genius of the Place," he reported in *The Spectator*, "and only made use of so much art as is necessary to help and regulate Nature without reforming her too much." *The Spectator* was widely read in Paris, and Rousseau was to be profoundly influenced by Addison's ideas. Addison's description of his own garden at Bilton Grange, where a foreigner knowing nothing of the English countryside might have "looked upon it as a natural wilderness," sounds very much like Rousseau's description of a natural garden landscape in *Héloise*.

In her discussion concerning the origins of the English landscape garden, Susi Lang has called attention to the possible influence of Alberti's writing, which continued to be universally read and studied in France, as well as in England. In these passages, Alberti seemed to foreshadow both Addison's essays on the imagination, as well as providing a blueprint for the landscape garden:

> But nature generally offers more conveniences, . . . for adorning the situation than the region; for we very frequently meet with cir- cumstance extremely noble and surprising, such as Promontories, Rooks, broken Hills . . . high and sharp, grottoes, caverns, springs and the like, near which, if we would have our Situation strike the Beholders with Surprise, we may build to our Heart's desire.[12]

Lang also pointed out the relevance of French treatises on landscape painting which were also very influential at the moment that the "Great Garden Revolu- tion" was beginning to gather steam in England, and to be followed shortly in France. In Henri Testelin's treatise, *The Sentiments of the Most Excellent Painters Concerning the Practice of Painting*, first published in France in 1680 and later translated into English in 1688, he set out for the student painter certain broad divisions of "Uninhibited places, where we have the liberty of representing all the extravagant effects of Nature, and the confused products of an uncultivated Land, in an irregular, but pleasant disposition."[13]

Artists in both France and England were even more thoroughly acquainted with Roger de Piles's *Cours de Peinture*, first published in 1708. In the English translation appearing in 1743, he discussed the elements of the "heroick" and pastoral styles of landscape. "The heroick style is a composition of objects, which in their kinds draws, both from art and nature, everything that is great and extraordinary in either." De Piles then proceeded to give a formula that could have been followed by the Comte d'Albon's gardens described in the Paris guidebook. "The situations are perfectly agreeable and surprising. The only buildings are temples, pyramids, ancient places of burial, altars consecrated to the divinities, pleasure-houses of regular architecture . . ." As for the pastoral style, in contrast to the heroic, the main element should be "openings or situations, accidents, skies and clouds, offskips and mountains, verdure or turfing, rocks, grounds . . . Buildings in general are a great ornament," he continues, "even if they are Gothick, or appear partly inhabited and partly ruinous; they raise the imagination by the use they are thought to be designed for."[14] De Piles went on to recommend mixing the various styles of landscape, thus bringing his work even closer to the Rococo landscape gardens then beginning to appear in elaborate asymmetricality in England during the 1720s. This transitional style was best illustrated in Stephen Switzer's *Iconographia Rustica* published in 1718, where the earliest surviving irregular garden plans first appeared. Switzer's garden designs had a great deal in common with the later French compositions of the *Jardin Anglais* with their quirky, twisting paths running through scenes of calculated variety.

De Piles's text was also closely related to the new interest in landscape painting that was beginning to appear in France, and through the works of such artists as Watteau, Joseph Vernet, and Hubert Robert. In the seventeenth century, landscape painting in France was not highly esteemed except as the setting or background for some human activity. As late as 1719 the Abbé Dubois in his "Critical Reflections on Poetry and Painting" condemned all landscape painting no matter how beautiful, or even if it was by Titian or Carracci, for "it is of no more interest to us than an actual tract of country, which may be either hideous or pleasant. Such a painting contains nothing which, as it were, speaks to us . . . Intelligent artists have always been so well aware of this truth that they have rarely painted landscapes without figures."[15]

French landscape painting in the seventeenth century was deeply affected by Dutch and Flemish artists, and their influence continued into the eighteenth century, inclining painters such as Watteau, Boucher, Oudry, and Desportes toward a greater realism in drawing nature and often in sketching directly, as they did at Montmorency and Arcueil. It is probably from examples of Dutch and Flemish, as well as from Italian painting, that French artists also developed a taste for the rustic, picturesque farm scene of thatched cottages and barns (Fig. 125). In the later part of the century, actual working farms would be incorporated into idealized landscape parks, as at Ermenonville, or built as romantic stage sets like Marie Antoinette's folly at the Petit Trianon. At *Moulin Joli*, Watelet's friend Boucher remodeled an existing farmhouse into a picturesque *maison bourgeois*, maintaining the utmost simplicity and recalling northern pastoral landscapes which he had both collected and copied as an aspiring artist.

French artists who could work in Italy discovered the importance of landscape painting in other countries, and were also introduced to a new vocabulary of picturesque subjects where ancient ruins, fragments of antique sculpture, and fountains in neglected parks evoked a romantic vision of the past. The hazy Roman landscapes of Fragonard, steaming with sexual promise amidst mysterious shadows, are recalled again and again in his views of the old French formal gardens overrun and abandoned (Fig. 126). Artists such as Watteau, who hadn't studied in Italy, but who were familiar with Italian drawings and paintings, began to discover a similar beauty and mystery in the Luxembourg and the overgrown gardens of Montmorency. The mature gardens, now grown to an arching, green freedom, were metamorphosed into a new fantasy of nature's disguise. Again, theatrical conventions were involved and can be seen in some of Watteau's paintings, where the illusion of the dream world of the garden is actually created in some of his works through his use of painted theater backdrops depicting Italian garden settings instead of actual views of the French gardens themselves, which had become more and more indistinguishable from the Italianate stage props. "Watteau's trees are copied from those of the Tuileries and Villas near Paris," Walpole perceptively observed, and appeared "like scenes of an opera. Fantastic people! Who range and fashion their trees, and teach them to hold up their heads, as a dancing-master would, if he expected Orpheus should return to play a minuet to them." While Claude and Poussin are most often mentioned as painters with the greatest influence on the English picturesque garden, it is interesting to note the recollection of Watteau as well. There is in Walpole's letters that delightful description of the fête given by Miss Pelham at Esher where the

125

126

127

ladies formed a circle before a cave "overhung to a vast height with woodbines, lilacs and laburnums, and dignified by tall shapely cypresses. On the descent of the hill were placed French horns; the abigails, servants and neighbors wandering below by the river; in short, it was Parnassus, as Watteau would have painted it."

Jean-Baptiste Oudry (1686–1755), too, had discovered a natural "studio" like Watteau's retreat at Montmorency, in the garden of the Prince de Guise at Arcueil. With his special privilege of entry, he was able to invite younger artists such as Portail, Boucher, and Natoire to join him there for instruction, and to follow his example by sketching the neglected grounds and crumbling architecture. Later in the century Hubert Robert could easily respond to the Roman "ruin pieces" of G. P. Panini, as a result of his familiarity with Oudry's circle, allowing him to combine both the antique and the picturesque without sentimentality and to translate something of that same quality into his concept of landscape garden design later in the century. When he returned from Italy in 1765 he visited his friend Watelet , where Boucher was working with him on his new "natural" garden, and there sketched the mill in the newly laid-out *Moulin Joli* (Fig. 127).

As the invigorating discovery of "the joys of nature" grew and spread throughout the century, the influence of Watteau, Oudry, Lancret, Hubert Robert, and Fragonard not only encouraged and helped to shape a new garden ideal in France, but throughout the rest of Europe as well. London as well as Rome attracted many French artists. Watteau worked in England in 1719, and his work was admired and collected at the very moment when the search for a more natural approach to garden design was getting underway. Addison's declaration that he preferred to "look upon a tree in all of its abundance and diffusions" than to see one that was "cut and trimmed into a mathematical perfection" was a sentiment widely shared by a new generation of French artists, and celebrated in their works. Addison's startling observation that he preferred the entertaining fancy and "artificial rudeness" of Italian and French gardens to the neat formality of English gardens at the beginning of the eighteenth century, may well have been because the same romantic gardens that Watteau painted had also appealed to the English essayist when he visited Paris.

Jean-Jacques Rousseau's mighty doctrine of the sacredness of nature in her purest form undoubtedly was indebted to Addison's essays. They had appeared in French versions as early as 1720. The famous garden in the *Nouvelle Héloise*, where Julie takes her lover Saint-Preux, is a wilderness in which all art is carefully concealed, recalling Addison's own "wild" garden which he described as being full of flowers growing in their natural state, and where the winding paths were covered with all kinds of climbing vines that spread along a meandering brook.

Foreshadowed by the enthusiastic reception of the Abbé Pluche's *The Spectacle of Nature* in 1732, and James Thomson's *Seasons* even earlier, in 1730, Rousseau's novel (published in 1761) was to have a deep and profound effect on French sensibility and the development of the radical new style of gardening *à le goût Anglo-Chinois*. Appropriately enough the celebrated garden in *Héloise* was owned by an Englishman who advocated the revolutionary notion that a garden could be anything but formal and symmetric, and that a whole garden could be laid out along natural, asymmetric lines. Rousseau even borrowed the anecdote from Beat de Muralt's *Lettres sur les Anglais et les Français* that when Le Nôtre was summoned to London by Charles II to redesign St. James Park, he had declared that he could not possibly improve on its noble simplicity and had, therefore, declined the commission!

The formal garden, like the formal house and palace in the seventeenth century, reflected a society's structure based upon the concept of an absolute monarchy. The French garden, as an extension of society's hierarchy of organization projecting the higher order of the state ordained by God onto the landscape, was so intimately tied to the prevailing style of classic architecture that it is not surprising to find the first literary descriptions of an alternative visual concept, as in Rousseau, to be isolated, wild parks without any architecture at all. Rousseau had, in fact, advocated the creation of natural parks and gardens devoid of any architectural elements which might betray the hand of man.

Practically speaking, the new informal garden scheme posed the very real problems of how to integrate a natural, asymmetrical landscape design with the formal requirements of an architecture which had not undergone a similar conceptual revolution, and thus continued to dictate the plan of its surroundings through the extension of formal, geometric lines. It was this seemingly unresolvable problem that perpetuated the use of the architectural forms of the parterres and straight walks near the house as the only possible setting for a formal house. The problem remained unresolved even in England, where as late as 1794, Humphrey Repton wrote in his *Sketches* that "Symmetry is also allowable and indeed necessary at or near the front of a regular building." In the designs for the garden of the Petit Trianon, the first plan showed the conventional geometric parterres acting as the transition into surrounding informality. These were later swept away in an attempt to accommodate the formal building within the indeterminate, informal landscape (Fig. 128 and Fig. 129).

The first irregular French gardens seem to have been attached to an existing formal scheme, but at a distance from the château or pavilion as a kind of a novel surprise hidden away in a corner or as an exotic "delight" concocted to replace an earlier *bosquet*. "There is a Monsieur Boutin," Horace Walpole reported from Paris to friends in England, "who has tacked [on] a piece of what he calls an English garden . . . There are three or four very high hills, almost as high as and exactly the shape of a tansy pudding." As French garden planners, patrons, and theorists struggled with the meaning and applications of the new philosophy, all manner of solutions combining both formal and "picturesque" elements were tried. While the results were sometimes amusing and bizarre, they often resulted in intimate gardens of remarkable Rococo charm and sentiment. One can still see something of this special, refined quality in corners of the English gardens at Chantilly, Rambouillet, and, most notably, in the English park of the Petit Trianon commissioned by Marie Antoinette in 1774 (Fig. 130 and Fig. 131). By that time the early Rococo gardens in England had been largely replaced by the landscape garden through the influence of Capability Brown and his followers. As a result, English travelers in the late eighteenth century were quick to point out how little the so-called English garden in France with its Rococo conceits resembled the real thing as conceived by Brown. Arthur Young stopped at Chantilly in 1787 and recorded that "the *hameau* contains an imitation of an English garden; the taste is but first introduced in France, so that it will not stand a critical examination."[16] Young later expressed the hope that "the winding walks and ornamented with a profusion of temples, benches, grottos, columns, ruins and I know not what" would not be thought to be in the English taste. "It is in fact as remote from it as the most regular stile of the last age."[17]

In his *Theorie der Gartenkunst*, published in 1779, C. C. L. von Hirschfield with penetrating insight, though with none of Walpole's wit, thoroughly scored the Anglomania that had been carried to excess by Frenchmen rushing to create gardens based on the imperfectly understood English models.

> In their blind imitation of the English taste they only repeat its faults, but also add new ones of their own. Everything that a large park can contain is crowded into an area not exceeding half an acre. Everything that Asia can offer in the way of new varieties of trees must be copied on the spot . . . Chinese monstrosities and kiosks, which are among the freakish features of the new extravagant architecture, oust the pure simplicity of Greek architecture . . . The new layouts are crowded with works of art of every kind, such as different sorts of buildings, ruins, bridges and so on; the feeling for what is simple and natural seems to have been entirely lost.[18]

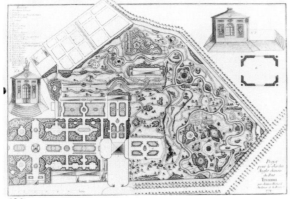

128

129

130

131

Hirschfield's attack echoes Rousseau's footnote in *Héloise* where he comments that he is "convinced the time is at hand when we shall no longer have in gardens anything that is found in the country." Aside from a taste for the cluttered, sentimental detail, the French suffered, as Hirschfield went on to point out, from a shortage of the English variety of natural topographies—at least in the environs of Paris—"of rich woods, mountains, rocks, springs and streams" for gardeners to exploit.

As for the Chinese influence in France, the English believed that it was a diplomatic ploy on the part of the French to adopt the Chinese myth, in order to mask French dependence on a style that was essentially English. But their belief was at least supported by the account of Yuan Ming-yuan, sent to Paris in 1745 by Père Attiret, who described how the old, formal gardens of China had been replaced by irregular schemes at the beginning of the eighteenth century. As early as 1690 Charles Dufresny, who had something of an irregular reputation as a garden designer, was impressed by earlier Jesuit reports of Chinese gardens, and Gabriel Thouin credits Dufresny with laying out the first free-form plan in the Faubourg Saint Antoine.

In his great series on the gardens of Europe, which he began to publish in 1776, George Le Rouge called the work *Details de Nouveaux Jardins à la Mode*. In the introduction, Le Rouge declared that all the world knew that the English garden was an imitation of the Chinese. In the *Gazette Littérraire* of 1771, a French writer observed that, although "Kent had the glory of being the first to introduce into his own country the most natural method of laying out gardens," the method had been invented "among the Chinese (and) the Japanese."[19] The Abbé Delille in a footnote to *Les Jardins* (1782) repeated the same genealogy.

In 1772–1773 a French edition of William Chambers's *A Dissertation on Oriental Gardening* appeared, extolling the achievement of the Chinese gardens and giving his account the added weight of presumably first-hand observations during a brief visit he had made to China in his youth. His description of gardens, consisting of a sequence of self-contained scenes, each calculated to stir the appropriate emotion, further encouraged the spread of the *Jardin Anglais* among the vaguely liberal and certainly fashionable leaders of French society who commissioned new gardens at an almost hysterical rate in the decades just before the Revolution. Le Rouge's plates attest to the extraordinary variety and number of these new Parisian gardens, undertaken by the rich bourgeois and members of the aristocracy with English tastes in the 1770s and 1780s, and far exceeding the development of urban gardens in and near London at the time.

Although Chambers emphasized the Chinese adherence to the model of nature, "collecting from nature the most pleasing objects" and combining them into an "elegant and striking whole" much like Western painters composing a picture, it is quite evident that the results were highly contrived and artificial. As if to further encourage the romantic visions of his readers, Chambers then completely contradicted himself by declaring that "the scene of a garden should differ as much from common nature, as an heroic poem doth from a prose relation: and gardeners, the poets, should give a loose rein to their imagination; and even fly beyond the bounds of truth wherever it is necessary to elevate, to embellish, to enliven or to add novelty to their subject."

With the growing "polyglot" vocabulary afforded by introducing English, Dutch, and Japanese garden styles and by erecting in three dimensions sublime scenes from the paintings of Salvator Rosa and Joseph Vernet, garden designers could become "practicing aesthetic psychologists" according to the emotions they orchestrated in their "pleasing," "terrible," or "surprising" garden pictures. In his autumnal garden, for example, Chambers recommended using decayed trees and dead stumps of picturesque forms combined with buildings and ruins that reek of "the disappointments and the dissolution of humanity," a formula followed in one contemporary French garden called a "Terrible Desert."

As for "surprising" scenes with supernatural elements to excite the spectator's imagination, Chambers introduced raging torrents at "the foot of impending rocks in the gloomy valleys." Dark passages with shadowy recesses reveal forms "which hold in their monstrous talons, mysterious cabalistic sentences inscribed on tables of brass." Further along, the exhausted visitor is revived "with repeated shocks of electrical impulse, with showers of artificial rain, or sudden violent gusts of wind and instantaneous explosions of fire." Chambers's soaring flights of imagination finally crossed the threshold of reality as he conjured up in his romantic excursions a poetic world of illusion far beyond the realm of any earthly garden.

The obsession with the idea of an escape into nature produced a whole new theater of experience centered on the garden, where enchanted scenes could be constructed out of the fields, woods, and streams of nature itself, or built to imitate nature in the secluded reaches of the parks of the old order. The sound effects of thunder and lightning that Chambers recommended for the garden were, in fact, common techniques widely used in eighteenth-century theaters. Similar theatrical techniques were also employed to create the *mise-en-scène* for the initiation ceremony of the Freemasons which was sometimes performed in a garden.[20]

Chambers's *Dissertation* has little to do with actual contemporary Chinese

132

gardens, with their rather limited and mediocre character, and the architect set off a storm of opposition in England led by Thomas Grey, Horace Walpole, and the poet William Mason, who satirized Chambers's ideas in verse. Nevertheless, his ideas, as well as his plans, for the first Chinese garden at Kew, built for the Duke of Kent (1750–1759), had a great effect throughout Europe—being taken up first in France where Chinese garden pavilions and pagodas began to appear in startling profusion (Fig. 132).

As a brake upon Chambers's overheated enthusiasm in linking the new garden style too closely to Chinese sources, Claude-Henri Watelet (1718–1786) published, in 1774, his *Essai Sur Les Jardins*, probably the first book of its kind to appear in French, although influenced by Thomas Whately's earlier English treatise. Watelet was a rich man who had inherited the privileges of farming taxes in the district of Orleans, thus enabling him to devote himself to art and literature. He was early associated with the Physiocrats and their utopian dreams of returning to a simple rural economy based on an idealized existence on a model farm, which he described in some detail in the *Essai*. As a young man he had traveled and sketched in Italy and later studied there with Hubert Robert. A surviving drawing of a bucolic farm scene reveals his taste for the picturesque, paralleling that of Oudry, Boucher, and Wille, complementing the ideal farm he outlines in the garden essay.

In 1760 he had been elected to the *Academie Française* on the strength of his didactic poem *L'art de Peindre*. Later he was to write articles on painting and engraving for the *Encyclopédie* and to indulge his interest in the theater by writing a short Italian pastoral drama called *Silvie*.

At the outset of his garden treatise Watelet declared his devotion to Rousseau's romantic nature philosophy and its fundamental importance to the aesthetic and psychological aspects of the art of gardening. Within the calm, soothing solitude of Rousseau's nature, "so favorable to arts and letters," friends united by their common devotion would find consolation and wisdom.

After discussing some of the more useful features of a garden—the orchards and vegetable gardens—he then proceeded with a detailed account of laying out a *ferme ornée* or small farm, where the fields and cultivated areas would be carefully composed for their aesthetic impact within an overall scheme. Even the barns, pig

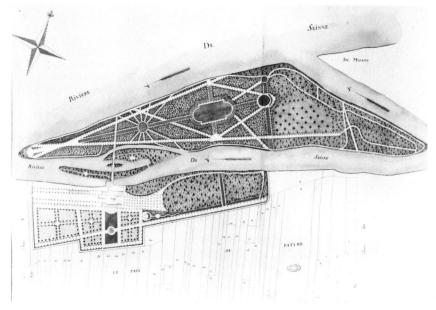

stys, and other lowly elements were subtly worked into a composition still meant
to function as an operating farm, concealing the artist's hand, in Rousseauesque
fashion, among the ducks and pigs, the meadows and the farm ponds. "Usefulness will be the foundation of my art," he righteously declared, "variety, order and
fitness will be its ornaments." In all of this Watelet showed his appreciation for the
picturesque landscape gardens of England, and especially the garden farm of the
poet William Shenstone, who laid out his famous miniature country estate, The
Leasowes, in 1745. Watelet seems to have followed Shenstone's original dictum
that "the garden is no longer limited to the place from which it takes its name, but
makes subject to its own laws both the laying out of a place and the embellishment
of the park, the farm, and the cart-track."

Watelet's ideal garden farm was based upon a personal experiment at his
island estate of *Moulin Joli à Colombes*, located on the edge of the Seine, not far
from Paris. Although the somewhat Rococo plan was dominated by a series of
straight lines of road network, the ground itself was quite irregular, and the
natural outline of the river bordered by wild trees and heavy undergrowth provided a picturesque setting unique in French gardens at the time it was created,
between 1754 and 1772 (Fig. 133).

Walpole, who visited "M. Watelet's isle" in 1775, entertained William Mason
with a first-hand, although waspish, account in the form of a "Jesuit Report" on
the recent conversion of the French to English gardening. Instead of finding "a
windmill made of ivory and inlaid with false stones" and "Dryads and Hama-
dryads gathering acorns in baskets of gauze," he discovered that M. Watelet had
"jumped back into nature, when she was not above nine hundred years old." And
in what could be taken as a familiarity with old overgrown formal gardens around
Paris—perhaps through painting as well as visits—Walpole went on to observe
that the "island differs in nothing from a French garden into which no mortal has
set foot for the last century."[24] The island was connected to the other part of the
estate by two bridges leading into "straight, narrow walks *en berceau* and surrounded by a rude path all around." In order to give the place a rural, rustic air, "a
plenary indulgence has been granted to every nettle, thistle and bramble that
originally grew in the garden of Eden." In spite of Watelet's elegant theories and
style in the *Essai*, Walpole concluded that his actual method of planning a garden
was much less studied. Watelet's recipe was simply to find a wilderness "full of

willows, cram it full of small elms and poplar pines, strip them into cradles, and cut them into paths, and have all the rest as rough as you found it, and you will have a *Moulin Joli*."

Two years before Watelet had begun his island garden, Jean-Francois Blondel had published his *Architecture Française* where he had distinguished different types of landscape problems such as the garden itself, the forest, and the woods. Blondel's description of a picturesque promenade consisting of "broad, interesting and varied points of view" among "beautiful disorder that produces valleys, hills, mountains . . . " anticipated the theories of Thomas Whately's *Observations on Gardening*, and may well have influenced Watelet's theory and practical work as well.

As for Chambers's praise of Chinese garden design, Watelet seems to have had some reservations, as the architect's theories and influence led to considerable exaggeration and unnecessary fussiness. France, he pointed out, was too removed from the Chinese, "a people living too far away and too different from ourselves," resulting in garbled accounts and myths regarding the exact nature of their celebrated gardens, which negated their usefulness as a model.

In the chapter on the origins of the "Great Garden Revolution" itself, and the French dependence on English precedence, he went on to characterize its chief aesthetic qualities as *le pittoresque, la poétique,* and *le romantique.* In the first category Watelet discussed composition, borrowing directly from painting, emphasizing again the link between painting theory and French landscape architecture in the second half of the eighteenth century. The other two characteristics reflected in the poetic and romantic scenes within the garden were compared by Watelet to scenes in the theater, which had been contrived to arouse the emotions and imagination without depending upon any dramatic action. Poetic associations were to be introduced into the landscape by art (statues) and architecture (temples and other structures of mythological or historical significance). Existing elements of nature freighted with psychological and sentimental associations, such as ancient trees, winding streams, and irregular ground — not to mention the primeval nettles, thistles, and brambles — were also to be incorporated into the composition, captivating both the eye and the imagination.

In a section on the "Materials Furnished by Nature," Watelet described the psychological qualities of the lawns, the woods, water, plants, the surrounding countryside itself, and even the empty space of the sky above.

Thomas Whately's influential *Observations on Gardening* published in Paris in 1771, three years before Watelet's *Essai*, contained a similar analysis. Water, having also been freed from the earlier geometric restraints of pools, basins, and canals, or use as a formal extension of sculpture in fountains, was especially singled out by Whately for its psychological and aesthetic values. "So various are the characteristics which water assume, that there is scarcely an idea in which it may not concur or an impression which it cannot enforce." Whately's emphasis was on the picturesque uses of water in the landscape and, extending his painterly theory, he called upon the gardener to use it in its most natural forms as streams, rivers, springs, and cascades that would appear to have been created by nature even when they were, in fact, artificial. The illusion of real water flowing through its natural bed or splashing down over rocks was to disguise all suggestion of artful creation.

Like Watelet, Whately also used theatrical analogies in discussing garden composition. In a "pastoral" passage, further extending the idea of garden landscape scenes as movable stage sets, he described a rocky Derbyshire valley where nature itself had produced the backdrop. The spectator "is enchanted by the perpetual shifting of scenes; the quick transitions; the total changes . . . , [T]he illuminated recesses, the fleeting shadows and the gleams of light glancing on the side, or trembling on the stream and the loneliness and stillness of the place all crowding together on the mind almost realize the ideas which naturally present themselves in the region of romance and fancy."[22]

When Louis Carrogis, known as Carmontelle (1717–1806), published his magnificent folio views of the *Jardin de Monceau*, a garden he had designed for the Duc de Chartres between 1773 and 1778, he prefaced the plates by saying that it was unnecessary to indulge in any theory since Whately's book had provided the last word. In the accompanying text, however, he did make a number of points. "If it is possible to transform a picturesque garden into a feigned landscape *(un pays d'illusions)* why should one not do so? Is it not illusions—if they are guided by Liberty and steered by art . . . that give us pleasure? . . . Let us introduce into our gardens the shifting scenes of the opera; let us represent in reality what the most skillful painters represent in their pictures."[23]

Inspired by Whately's treatise and following his own imagination, Carmontelle approached the creation of the *parc Monceau* with the express objective of constructing a "Garden of Illusion," of a theater where contrived elements would be presented as a vision of reality, of nature itself. Instead of the classical concept of the French garden in which the spectator could grasp the main scheme in the first encounter, the "Garden of Illusion" was designed to transport the visitor in time and space, traversing in a short stroll a whole series of stations of the imagination. Carmontelle's experiments with movable transparencies in a miniature stage illustrating a garden promenade as a "moving picture" may well have had an effect on his novel ideas of landscape composition.

If, as he suggested, Carmontelle had opera in mind when he planned Monceau, some of the actual harebrained results were closer to musical comedy. In a restricted suburban space, although larger than its much altered surviving form, Carmontelle managed to include an amazing variety of garden conceits. There was an Italian vinery and a miniature farm, harboring not only sheep and cows but a lone camel as well (Fig. 134). There was, of course, a Chinese section where servants in Chinese robes served refreshments and, like an international World's Fair, the nearby Turkish and Persian pavilions had their own exotically costumed attendants (Fig. 135). In the winter garden, a large grottolike room provided what must have been a very dark and dank place for supper parties (or initiation rites?) but relieved by "live" music piped in through channels in the ceiling from a secret chamber above, where the musicians played (Fig. 136).

Like the Duc de Chartres's Monceau, and many of the other gardens illustrated in Le Rouge, the inspiration and encouragement of the new garden styles came from a significant number of patrons, talented amateur designers who had flourished in the rich soil and leisured sunshine of the *ancien régime*. François Racine de Monville, with a large income and an insignificant post at court, for example, enjoyed the life of the arts as a musician and draftsman and knew many of the leading artists and landscape architects of the day. Madame de Genlis described him as a "great suitor, young, a widower, rich and very handsome, noble and romantic but not of the court."[24] In 1774 de Monville acquired a rugged, naturally picturesque piece of woods next to the old royal domain of Marly and there constructed over a period of ten years the so-called *Désert de Retz*, one of the most remarkable gardens of the eighteenth century (Fig. 137). Although assisted in the beginning by the architect Barbier, it is uncertain exactly whose hand was involved in the ultimate realization of the garden, and the construction of the famous Column House in 1780–1781. The influence of Hubert Robert and Étienne Boullée have been mentioned repeatedly but without any specific documentation. De Monville, like Chartres, was a prominent member of the Freemasons, and it has also been suggested that Masonic ritual and symbolism entered into the layout of both the Désert and Monceau. Rousseau had earlier proposed the natural landscape as the place for man to begin his regeneration, so that the use of de Monville's garden for the initiatory ritual of Freemasonry is quite plausible and would explain the ceremonial route connecting the various garden structures. The "primitive" form of the grotto entrance at the Désert might well be the starting

134

135

136

h. Lanternes K. Sallon dans les Roches, m. Soupiraux par lesquels on entend la Musique dans le Sallon, K.

Coupe du nouveau Berceau ou JARDIN D'HIVER de S.A.S.M. le Duc de Chartres à Mousseau par la ligne A.B. du plan.

Place des Musiciens

Cabinet

A   B

La MAISON du DÉSERT de Mr de Monville

The HOUSE of the DESERT, belonging to Mr de Monville   Hrn von Monville's HAUS gennant le DESERT

137

point through the ritual of traversing the history of civilization via the forms of architecture, beginning in the cave and ending in a temple of utopian dreams (Fig. 138).

If one entered the park through a heavy rusticated gate on the forest side, the opposite face of the entrance turned out to be the opening of a grotto built of loose stones piled up as a natural rockery. The opening was guarded and illuminated by torch-bearing satyrs placed on either side. A drive wound down the natural slope, past a pyramid that served as an icehouse and on to the center compositional piece, a gigantic broken column of the Tuscan order embedded in the side of the hill. Inside its fluted plaster walls was concealed an elegant house of five main floors, the residence of the owner. The Prince de Ligne, himself a garden amateur of note, remarked that it looked like the fragment of a colossal temple which, like the Tower of Babel, had suddenly called down upon itself the wrath of God.

The use of the circular form of the Column House was, in fact, a brilliant solution to the vexing problem of uniting architecture with a sensuous, irregular landscape composition, and eliminating all of the sharp, geometric angles of the classic French châteaux and pavilions. The winding walks could encircle and converge upon the central feature without any forced transition through the conventional architectural garden setting as, for example, at nearby Bagatelle, where the formal lines of the pavilion sharply confronted the surrounding English park.

The Désert's apparently ancient ruin of a small Gothic Chapel was so cleverly incorporated into the scheme that one is not sure of its age. In another corner of the park is the so-called Temple of Pan, and below it was located the now-vanished *Maison Chinoise*. From the drawings (see Fig. 132) it is apparent that the designer had no real Chinese model in mind, for only the ornamentation of the essentially French structure suggested an oriental connection.

Between the *Maison Chinoise* and the Column House an amphitheater was created on the slope simply by defining the apron of the stage through the use of a stone terrace flanked by two ornamental urns on either side (Fig. 139). The audience, already a part of a dramatic setting created by the theatrical props of the garden itself, viewed the productions from below the terrace facing back toward the truncated column romantically forming a permanent backdrop in the distance (Fig. 140).

The theater of the Désert de Retz was similar in design and scale to the theater at the Château Abondant not far from Anet and built in the 1750s by Nicholas Michot (1707–1790). Abondant's theater was enclosed by palisades of green hedge, and the permanent stage flats placed to accelerate the perspective on either side were also formed by trimmed banks of hornbeam.[25] A similar theater was planned for Marie Antoinette at Trianon (Fig. 141). At the Désert the scene projecting into the garden was composed as a corner of nature where large trees flaunted their branches over the playing area as living stage sets, while trying to conceal their theatrical function and become a part of the garden composition.

Throughout the latter half of the eighteenth century we are repeatedly faced with subtle illusions and manipulation of reality in the French garden. Real trees became stage props, and artificial lakes became rivers. Unexpected tensions were produced through the juxtaposition of disparate elements, as in the primitive grotto and exotic assembly of trees and plants surrounding Ledoux's Hôtel Thélusson, with its monumental classic entry arch designed to serve as a proscenium frame for the public audience passing in the streets nearby (Fig. 142). Or compare, for example, the living stage set of trees at the Désert de Retz with the *treillage* in the form of a triumphal arch in the garden of M. de la Bossiere and illustrated in Le Rouge. Here the illusion of the Désert's theater was reversed, and, instead of seeing real trees and countryside incorporated into the garden theater, we are confronted with a painted *trompe-l'oeil* scene of wilderness, jagged rocks, and a disappearing stream seen within the arched openings of the trellis, recalling the painted perspective of the triumphal arch in Richelieu's garden at Rueil (Fig. 143).

The famous *Hameau* of Marie Antoinette, consisting of a group of fake Norman farm buildings, of course, falls into the category of the garden stage set. The initial inspiration probably came from Dutch and Flemish genre paintings and the obsession with creating any kind of scene in the garden that could be considered "picturesque." It was also a result of the influence of Rousseau, Watelet, and the philosophers advocating the virtues of the simple natural life, whose ideas were translated into sham villages for the fashionable client who wanted any radical notions coopted into innocent forms of pleasure and ingenious decoration.

Théâtre Decouvert sous un Berceau de Grands Ormes.

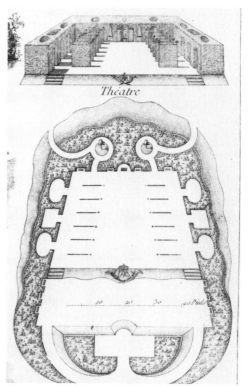

Théatre

140

141

The interior of these rustic pavilions, with their *trompe-l'oeil* exterior walls, were frequently decorated in the most startling manner and one of exotic richness. The tiny jewel rooms of the rustic thatched cottage at Rambouillet, the *Chaumière de Coquillage,* were completely covered with the most intricate and refined shell work, inlaid in delicate mosaic (Fig. 144). Among Le Rouge's plates there is a plan for a garden farm building, complete with an inviting hay loft suitable for amorous rompings. When the door was opened, however, as if one had stumbled upon a vision in a magic forest created by the Brothers Grimm, the unsuspecting visitor was confronted with the interior of a richly appointed tent such as that of a Roman general on an Eastern campaign, embellished with banners, armour, and other antique military appointments (Fig. 145 and Fig. 146).

The earliest plan to transform the park surrounding Gabriel's classic Petit Trianon into an informal garden of intricately winding paths, canals, and curving lakes dated from 1774, and was done for Marie Antoinette by Antoine Richard, *Jardinier de la Reine*. A later modification by Richard Micque illustrated the further simplification of the design into more open lawns and well-defined tree clumps (see Fig. 128 and Fig. 129). The Queen's interest in the new garden style was apparently genuine, for she visited many of the most recent garden creations around Paris, including the Count d'Artois's Bagatelle, actually built as a result of a bet with the Queen. Its grounds had been laid out by the Count's crusty Scotch gardener, Thomas Blaikie, who once enjoyed a long talk with the Queen about gardening during one of her visits. Blaikie worked with the French architect François-Joseph Belanger (1744 – 1818), who had traveled widely in England, studying first-hand the English art of landscape and sketching garden architecture — although the two did not always agree on garden design principles. Blaikie's dogmatic taste was reflected in his insistence upon large open spaces of greensward, Brownian clumps of trees, and the singling out of individual tree specimens as a focal point. He also introduced a wide variety of rare plants from

142

143

144

EXTERIEUR
de la Chaumiere
du Jardin Anglais
à M. le Comte d'Harcourt
à Chaillot.
A PARIS
Chez le Rouge.

145

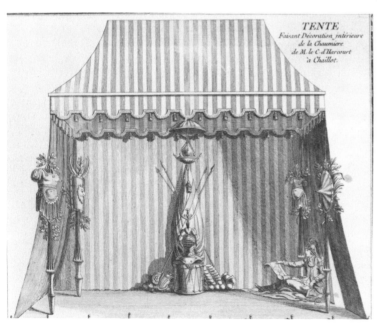

TENTE
Fasant Décoration intérieure
de la Chaumiere
de M. le C. d'Harcourt
à Chaillot.

146

foreign countries into his gardens, a feature that had become widespread in many of the more fashionable layouts. In his diary Blaikie was always criticizing the clutter and confusion that seemed to prevail in the new gardens, such as Monceau, and he was particularly sensitive to the problems of linking architecture to its surroundings. The French, he noted in his diary, "look upon a house and a garden as two objects that do not correspond with the other," and he cited the example of Bagatelle where the house was surrounded by a wall ten feet high. When he proposed removing it, "to give an open elegance to the house and join the Gardens," he met strong opposition (Fig. 147).[26]

Close to d'Artois's Bagatelle, Claude Baudard de Saint-James set out with the express ambition of overshadowing his royal neighbor's garden, and commissioned Belanger to undertake the work. Blaikie also provided some advice and assistance, but he was not impressed with this extravagant and eccentric project, which finally ruined Saint-James. Water was raised by a steam pump to form a large, artificial lake scene, but the finest element was Belanger's great rock grotto, where water gushed forth below the portico of a Doric temple in the center of the gigantic rock cave (Fig. 148). Belanger's original intention was to have the water fall from the center of the arch in a sheet down the front of the portico. Behind the grotto in the hill was a room furnished as a bath. When it was completed, the *Folie de Saint-James*, with its profusion of temples, bridges, and watercourses, was indeed the most extravagant private park built during the last, disintegrating years of the old order (Fig. 149).

By far the greatest concentration of examples of the new garden style — Chinese, English, or a riotous combination of picturesque and literary inspirations —was in and around Paris itself. The capital, for all of the well-known historical, political, and cultural reasons, held its citizens in thrall, and, even after the bondage of Versailles was broken, there was no wholesale rush to distant country estates during the eighteenth century. The well-defined boundary of the small urban garden or estate, with its predictable limits, helped to increase a Rococo density in an artificial wilderness confined by city streets and walls. Even though paeans were offered to the liberated wonders of nature, the actual intention of French landscape architects working in Paris in the later half of the century was to pile up a rich visual, emotional, and intellectual experience within a fairly small space, and the irregular town lots offered opportunities for ingenious garden solutions. The long, narrow form of Beaumarchais's garden is a *tour de force* of the romantic style carried out on a most unpromising urban site (Fig. 150). Heavy screens of trees and treillage preserved a private, intimate quality. These barriers and walls formed "light corridors and transpicuous arbours," Walpole noted with unaccustomed approval, "through which the sun-beams play and chequer the shade, set off the statues, vases and flowers, that marry with their gaudy hotels, and suit the gallant and idle society who paint the walks between their parterres and realize the fantastic scenes of Watteau and Durfé."[27] Even when large open spaces were available, as at Maisons, where Belanger was asked to lay out a new English garden, only four or five acres, according to Blaikie, were actually used. This parsimonious response to the expansive and beautiful view of the river disgusted Blaikie, who found French landscape ideas hopelessly "contracted."

Blaikie's sympathies were firmly in the camp of the English picturesque school when he told the superintendent at Maisons that "the whole ground round the house ought to correspond else they never could think of having anything beautiful but this they had no idea of."[28] It was a blunt Scottish paraphrase of Addison's rhetorical question posed in *The Spectator* in 1712. "Why may not a whole Estate," he asked, "be thrown into a kind of garden by frequent Plantations. A man might make a pretty Landskip of his own Possessions." The answer to Addison's question was given with relentless energy in England in the latter half of the eighteenth century under the leadership of Capability Brown. The natural English countryside, with its intensified farming methods, readily lent

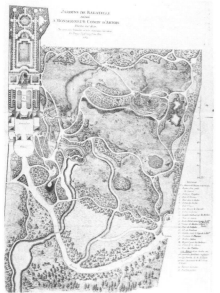

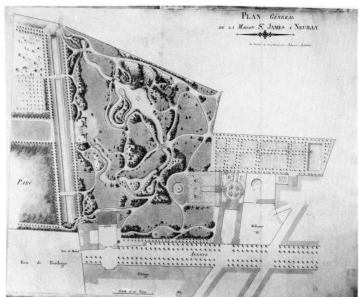

147

149

148

itself to the new landscape style in a way that seemed impossible in France, where feudal agricultural practices had not shaped the fields and meadows with a comparable harmony.

In the preface to his English translation of the essay of the Marquis de Girardin, whose elegant treatise championed the picturesque garden, Daniel Malthus remarked upon the "cheerless plains of France" which, he explained, referred to "the vast fallows that disgust the eye of the stranger," due to the antiquated farming methods and wasteful use of land.[29] Earlier in the 1730s, the Abbé Le Blanc, who visited England and noted the English gardens in his letters, was also struck by the natural beauty of the surrounding landscape that complemented the great parks. . . . [T]he care with which the country is cultivated," he wrote, "is a consequence of the plenty in which the farmer lives."[30] "It is a peasant's landscape," Henry James noted even a century and a half later as he drove through France, "not as in England, a landlord's."

The Marquis de Girardin, a student and friend of Rousseau and a dedicated Anglophile, had begun in the 1760s, with the help of the garden architect J. M. Morel, to transform his estate north of Paris, Ermenonville, into a picturesque park. Near the end of Rousseau's life, Girardin invited the famous philosopher to come and live with him in his new Arcadia, where the writer fortuitously died, providing Girardin with the supreme opportunity for a romantic landscape enthusiast to erect in his own garden a tomb-shrine in honor of the founder of the nature cult.

In his *De la Composition des paysages*, published in 1777, Girardin forcefully set out his ideas "on the means of improving and embellishing the countryside round our habitations," principles he had actually followed at Ermenonville. Like Stourhead in Wiltshire, the highly programmed park was centered upon an irregular body of water, although in a more extensive and illusive configuration which combined both a long, sensuous lake and an artificial river. The scheme was cut in two by an ancient château which Girardin had modernized, throwing its dilapidated moat into the surrounding water garden. Blaikie thought the only good place to see the park was from the château itself, since that was the only viewing point from which it would not be visible.

Girardin took as his point of departure Rousseau's *Nouvelle Héloise*, laying out winding paths around the lake, but linked together in an un-Rousseauian fashion by a series of prospects and structures loaded with associative views intended to recall the works of admired painters. Throughout his essay Girardin continually referred to the parallels between garden composition and painting. Like the painter, the landscape designer was to approach the problems of composition not merely by resorting to irregularity and caprice, but through imagination and study of the topography. The plan for the garden, following the analogy of the artist's preparatory sketch, was to be complete at the outset. In his recommendations

150

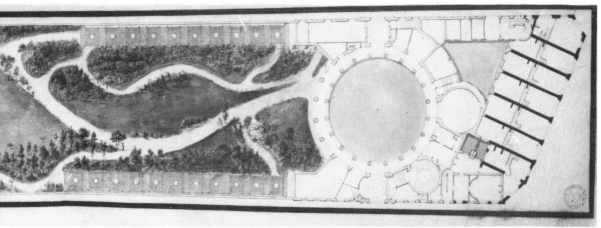

concerning the necessity of having a professional landscape painter "who is not too narrow in his school" close at hand to copy the designer's plan, Girardin confronted one of the dilemmas of laying out an informal scheme. The question was, as Susi Lang has put it, "How does a gardener actually lay out a landscape garden that has to be planned in the three dimensions of an open landscape, often on an uneven ground, over hills and dales?"[31] The school of Le Nôtre could simply resort to paper, pen, and ruler. The Marquis, in fact, claimed that part of the success of the formal school was due to sheer laziness, because it was so much easier to concentrate on paper than to actually confront and critically examine the natural topography — to "consult the Genius of the Place" before beginning. Certainly the spread of the formal style was, in part, due to the exact planning formulas, such as those of d'Argenville and Le Blond, who were able to reduce the methods of planning procedure to a compact set of rules easily followed. Even when the "natural" style clearly demanded other techniques, it was difficult for French architects and designers to give up their traditional methods for a more intuitive, imaginative approach. Blaikie reports the astonishment of the French workmen at Bagatelle when he traced out the basic plan of the garden on the ground "without line or *tois.*"[32]

Girardin thought that a professional painter should actually accompany the garden designer as he walked over the site, analyzing and composing his prospects. Since the Marquis was aware of the theory of stage design and its use in garden planning, the creation of the illusion of distance, while still presenting a unified view, called for theater techniques which the artist could also provide. The use of illusion to create a sense of distance in a garden was really a money saver, Girardin declared, because it spared one from having to buy up vast quantities of adjoining land, simply for effect. Preliminary sketches were to be in pencil, so they could be corrected, representing only the outlines of the principal objects and the disposition of large masses. After the sketch had been adjusted and corrected, the painter could then make a finished landscape painting to guide the actual work.

In laying out the composition on the ground, Girardin recommended that the side scenes, as on a stage, be established first by massed woods, to form the perspective. Outlines of buildings and structures should be indicated by building temporary frames to scale, and covering them with canvas. Water compositions were to be tested by spreading out the canvas over the proposed site.

In a chapter called "On the connection with the Country," the Marquis, recalling Addison's recommendations in *The Spectator*, devoted great attention to harmonizing the garden and park with its surroundings, relating colors, shapes, and even the textures of plant materials within the controlled area to the open country outside. "If it is a corn country, you cannot possibly connect it with your ground unless you make part of your ground the same color with the surrounding fields and give the same appearances of cultivation."[33] Distant villages and farms should also be brought into "the garden picture." As for painters whose works should be included in a landscape "museum without walls," he recommended Poussin, Bourdon, Rubens, Claude, Richard Wilson, John Smith, Gaspar Duget (Poussin), Francisco Zuccarelli, Salvator Rosa, Paul Brill, Antoine Watteau, Nicolas Bergham, Paul Potter, and Tenier the Younger.

Girardin includes the poet along with the painter as a prime collaborator in any serious garden planning, and this was evidenced at Ermenonville with lines of poetry displayed throughout the park. The so-called "Obelisque Pastoral" held plaques to the apostles of nature romanticism, and quotations from classical authors. Carved on a block near the obelisk was a poem in homage to William Shenstone, the English gardener who had written his own guide to landscape gardening at the Leasowes in elaborate verse. Girardin had visited the Leasowes in the 1760s and had found its simplicity much more to his taste than the grandeur of Blenheim and Stowe. Girardin's treatise was, in fact, more closely related to Shenstone's essay than any contemporary French garden writing, although

Ermenonville's great size and its use of architecture was a major departure from Shenstone's model.

Along with the temples, towers, altars, grottos, and cascades there were also rustic huts and a primitive bridge at Ermenonville. Primitive forms of architecture reflecting the origins of the art fascinated many eighteenth-century theorists, inspired by Rousseau's speculations concerning the root of other social and behavioral phenomenon. In fact, the form of the First House had haunted nearly everyone concerned with architecture going as far back as Vitruvius in the first century B.C. Where but in a garden, a paradise on earth, could the question be explored and models tested—or so it would seem from the number of projects for primitive garden structures. The Abbé Laugier, in his *Essai Sur l'Architecture*, illustrated his theory with a shelter of four upright trees supporting a pitched roof covered with leaves. From this simple structure, argued Laugier, all later architecture had evolved. Laugier's hut was not unlike those of William Chambers, who also provided plans and elevations for garden huts. Because of the freedom afforded the architect's imagination within the picturesque garden landscape, primitive pavilions turn up in many late eighteenth-century gardens, where a kind of experimental, *avant garde* atmosphere was encouraged by the "natural" setting and by the often liberal-minded gentleman-patron, like Girardin, who was fashionably interested in advanced architectural theories (Fig. 151 and Fig. 152).

Having called upon all of the historic influences on French garden design over the centuries — painting, poetry, theater, architecture — Girardin the romantic humanist did not forget music, an essential part of the French garden experience, as natural as the trees, water, flowers, and rocks. "The walks in the garden which offer so many lovely views," a visitor to Ermenonville wrote, "are not only intended for the eye, but also for the ear; for the marquis de Girardin employs a number of skillful musicians, who perform not only in the castle itself, but also out in the woods, on the shores of the lake or on the water, either several together or singly. Nowhere does one find such naturalness . . ." (Fig. 153).[34]

If Girardin's essay had been the most effective summary of the principles of the French version of the picturesque park, Jean-Joseph de Laborde's great park of Méréville was, without doubt, the finest interpretation of those principles. The estate of over nine thousand acres, where an old castle looked out over a wild, swampy valley watered by the river Juine, was acquired by Laborde in 1784. The precipitous hills, the brooding groves of overgrown trees in the valley and, above all, its monumental scale, like a painting of Claude, sent the imagination winging back to the beginning of time. Only the tame, meandering river Juine was something less than one expected of a primeval stream, but this could be corrected and idealized by subtle art (Fig. 154).

The gigantic dimensions of Laborde's idealized visionary premises reflected a similar taste for the grandiloquent statement in architecture, as one sees in Piranesi's engravings and in the architectural works of Gondoin, Peyre, Boullée, and Ledoux. The cult of the colossal had been foreshadowed in Edmund Burke's definition of the Sublime and the Beautiful that rejected the Rococo conception of architecture and gardens as a sequence of well-bred, intimate, informal environments. The Rococo garden, as the Marquis de Girardin pointed out, had attempted to assemble "the production of all climates and monuments of all ages, bringing the whole world together" within its congested boundaries. The neoclassical artistic ideal, on the other hand, was to reduce forms to their primal purity, evoking the archaic world of timeless truths and limitless vistas, like the soaring view from Thomas Jefferson's Monticello in Virginia.

In order to purify nature and to give it the appropriate elements which would recall elegiac classical scenery, Laborde's efforts required the energy and organization demonstrated by Fouquet at Vaux-le-Vicomte more than a hundred years before. At a reported cost of millions, hundreds of workmen were employed to drain the swampy valley, to divert and "correct" the river, and to build entire

151

152

153

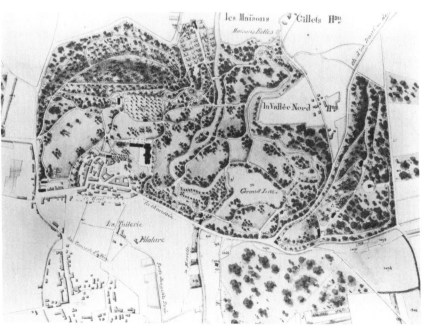

154

hillsides of new soil for trees wherever nature had been found wanting. The modest river was put into a new bed to improve its picturesque lines and to wind through the park, operating a mill on its course, then passing into a lake before it disappeared into a long subterranean channel—suddenly emerging again in a grotto and then falling down a magnificent cascade.

The aesthetics of water shaped by the new, romantic philosophy with its charged sensibilities once again dominated the garden composition at Méréville in a way that had not been seen since the great formal water garden creations of the previous century. The subtle play with the sound as well as the sight of water at Méréville, with all of its psychological and symbolic associations, was very much in that French tradition extending back to the earliest fountains and water displays. "On the one side the waterfall shuts out the view, and its continuous roar fills one's ears," reported a visitor. "If one now enters the adjacent grotto, one hears only a subdued murmur from the lovely cascade; and in the grotto one hears nothing at all; the impressions are varied by degrees" (Fig. 155).[35]

In order to give some scenic balance and scale to the almost overwhelming presence of nature, and to control the perspectives over an unwieldy space, Laborde called in Hubert Robert and Belanger to set the "pictures" within the overall composition, as well as to design the architectural elements. Hubert Robert had been named garden designer to Louis XVI in 1778 and had contributed to garden projects at Versailles, Trianon, and Rambouillet. As a friend of Watelet and Girardin, he had also been involved with two of the key figures in the French picturesque garden revolution, although it is not clear what precisely he may have contributed to *Moulin Joli* or Ermenonville. His new installation at Versailles of the Apollo group originally created for Louix XIV's *Grotte de Thétis*, however, was a bold, successful invasion of Le Nôtre's formal scheme, just north of the *Parterre de Latone* (Fig. 156). Belanger had carried out major garden commissions at Bagatelle and the *Folie de Saint-James*. He had also studied at first-hand some of the great English landscape gardens, making notes and sketches of Stowe, Stourhead, Wilton, the Leasowes, Fonthill, Claremont, Hagley, and Painshill during his visit in 1777-1778.

Except for the old château, which was remodeled and extended along the ridge above the valley, Laborde and his collaborators apparently inherited little in the way of earlier landscape structure to interfere with the new plans. In the true spirit of the neoclassical age, after removing what was left of an older garden, all was reduced to a *tabula rasa* of luxuriant, archaic wilderness ready to inspire a new beginning. "One cannot create a garden without a little poetry," Belanger once wrote a prospective client, and it is clear that poetry as well as art were employed at Méréville. Belanger may well have had in mind the comments of the painter Salomon Gessner when he said that the great landscapes of Poussin and Claude owed their power and mobility to the poetic genius of the artists. Gessner's formula for a successful landscape painting anticipated Girardin's recommendations in his garden treatise. Nature itself had to be shaped and manipulated into a picturesque composition. The river, the lake, the grottos, the cascades, the waterfalls, even the "natural" bridge which appeared to have been formed by water over the millennia were subtle artistic deceptions at Méréville of art imitating nature in the garden composition (Fig. 157).

The philosophy and intention of providing the aesthetic and emotional experience of wild, natural scenery within the manageable and accessible confines and visible order of one's own garden was in spirit, at least, related to the garden philosophy of China. The use of art to reveal, as well as to enhance, the beauty of the hills, the river, the woods and, above all, the great natural rock constructions, suggested a strong oriental sympathy on the part of the creators of Méréville (Fig. 158).

In order to hold the distant groves and fields at bay and to impose order to the edges of the park, beyond the unity and continuity created by the river in its

Seconde Vue de la GRANDE CASCADE de MÉRÉVILLE.

Second View of the PRINCIPAL CASCADE at MÉRÉVILLE   Zweite Ansicht des GROSSEN WASERFALLES von MÉRÉVILLE

155

156

various guises, Laborde strategically positioned a number of classical temples and monuments. Opposite the château across the valley the most striking monument is the *Colonne Triumphal,* a directional signal rising to a height of thirty meters (Fig. 159). Another architectural monument commemorated the heroic explorations and death of Captain Cook, reminding the visitor of exotic travels to distant places, a standard element in garden design programs of the eighteenth century.

The Temple of Love, modeled after the famed Sibyl Shrine at Tivoli, stood originally on an island in the river and sheltered a statue of Laborde's daughter, sculpted by Pajou. Later it was moved to a more dramatic site on a hill recalling the ancient Italian scene which had inspired countless artists from Claude to Boucher and Hubert Robert (whose own painting of the Méréville setting makes clear the connection, even to the detail of the rustic footbridge) (Fig. 160 and Fig. 161).

The most imposing classical structure in Méréville's park was the so-called *laiterie* or dairy. It was taken down, along with the Temple of Love, and removed to a neighboring estate at the end of the last century. It originally served as the entrance to the grotto built into the hill behind. Within the cool inner grotto room formed from natural rocks, water from the diverted river reappeared to gush forth from a niche into a marble basin where the figure of Diana emerged from the bath. It was a noble, impressive tableau that must have rivaled in its original state the dairy at Rambouillet that had been designed for Marie Antoinette. (Fig. 162, Fig. 163, and Fig. 164.).

After flowing across the white marble floor of the grotto room of the dairy, the river vanished once again into its underground conduit only to suddenly reappear further along, but completely transformed into the roaring cascade falling down

VUE GÉNÉRALE du PARC de MÉRÉVILLE.

GENERAL VIEW of the PARK of MEREVILLE. ALLGEMEINE ANSICHT des PARKS von MEREVILLE.

157

158

Premiere Vue de la GRANDE CASCADE à Méréville.

First View of the GREAT CASCADE of Méréville. Erste Ansicht des GROSSEN WASSERFALLS zu Méréville

159

160

161

La LAITERIE à MÉRÉVILLE.

The DAIRY at MEREVILLE. MILCHKELLER zu MEREVILLE.

162

163

over a seemingly natural and sublime tumble of colossal rock that might have come from the painting of Joseph Vernet which decorated Laborde's dining room in the château (Fig. 165 and Fig. 166). The careful, almost oriental analysis of the elements of nature by French artists such as Vernet in the eighteenth century undoubtedly contributed to the freer and more imaginative handling of these garden constructions than could be observed in similar rock conceits in English parks such as Stowe, Stourhead, and Painshill.

Given the turning, winding course to which the river Juine had been subjected, bridges to connect the various scenes as "a moving picture," in the words of Belanger, were both a necessity and an opportunity. The bridge in the classical and picturesque countryside had, of course, been a ubiquitous feature in seventeenth and eighteenth-century paintings. In England the decorative garden bridge had become one of the chief architectural elements in the picturesque garden. The new interest in Chinese design simply enlarged the range of poetic styles available to the garden architect.

Belanger had actually used a bridge as a central element in the design of Beaumarchais's Paris garden, much as the seventeenth century had used terraces both to unify the composition and to provide an unexpected elevation for viewing the layout. Belanger saw the function of the garden bridge not only as a link in the

164

165

Grande Roche
d'Après Vernet

Autres, IDÉES
d'Après Nature

166

Pl. 56

L'ILE NATALIE à MÉRÉVILLE.

NATALY ISLAND at MEREVILLE. Die NATALIEN-INSEL zu MEREVILLE.

167

pictorial composition but as a means of enhancing the visual experience. Belanger's letter urging a client to build more bridges in her garden even invoked the sacred name of Milton; "In his wonderful description of the earthly Paradise, Milton speaks of a high bridge leading to a grove of myrtles" where "the birds made a melodious choir, and to which the breezes bore the fragrance from the flowers in the vales and thickets spanned by this bridge" (Fig. 167).[36]

Along one side of Méréville's domain the public road itself was blended imperceptibly into the overall design as it passed over a bridge spanning the exhausted river leaving the park, providing the public with a glimpse into Laborde's Elysium on either side. The road and bridge created a transitional passage in the composition by linking the contrived pastoral retreat with the outside, everyday public spaces. It was a delight and went beyond contemporary landscape practice, although the idea was central to Girardin's treatise on the integration of the garden and the countryside by using the road to obliterate the garden's walls.

In a chapter of his *Essai*, called "Of the Power of Landscape over the Senses, and through their Interposition over the Soul," Girardin made the metaphysical case for an earthly paradise like Ermenonville or Laborde's retreat. "In a situation of picturesque beauty, where nature unconfined displays all her graces," recalling "the scene of man's first happiness," the truth of the universe can be rediscovered. It is possible, even in an imperfect world, to "create anew by the hand of taste, an ideal setting, protected by natural ramparts of hills and mountains," a Golden Age "intended by nature as the last asylum of peace and liberty."

But even before the arcadian landscape at Méréville had been completed, the era of the garden as the "last asylum" was coming to a close. Future visions of paradise would be colored by the nineteenth-century spectrum of political and economic reform, of new states and new constitutions. Gardens like Rambouillet and Rainey would become botanical laboratories and scientific farms anticipating the nineteenth-century land grant colleges of the New World. Le Nôtre's *allées* would become visionary avenues in new cities in the wilderness, beginning with Washington. The ideal city itself was seen by artists such as Ledoux to be a great garden carved out of a sylvan river valley (Fig. 168). With the collapse of the *ancien régime* in 1789, the energy and imagination that had transformed ephemeral trees, plants, flowers, pavilions, and water into aesthetic masterpieces of landscape art would no longer be focused on nature's possibilities as merely gardens with the same vitality and spacious confidence.

In its supernatural space and majestic cadence, its hidden sanctuaries, the French garden held out the enticements of peace, happiness, and pleasure on this earth. Formal and articulate, or picturesque and illusory, it had combined art and nature into unforgettable apparitions of wonder and prophecy. But as a cerebral production, like an epic poem, such garden ideals no longer command our imagination, and their absence makes us the poorer, as Bartlett Giamatti has reminded us. In losing that Renaissance, that French breadth of understanding of nature transformed by rules and codes not only into epics but into an actual garden as a special place designed for our sensual and spiritual pleasure as art, "we have lost," in the words of Giamatti, "the unearthly paradise once again not only as a state of joy but also as an object of hope."[37]

VUE PERSPECTIVE DU PONT DE LA LOUE.

Caption Notes *Chapter V*

Fig. 121—*"Carmontelle remettant les clefs du Monceau au Duc de Chartes."* The artist and the duke are on the left in the overloaded setting of visual anecdote. (Musée Carnavalet)

Fig. 122—*"La Perspective."* Watteau's painting of the garden of Le Brun's Montmorency (Fig. 115) reveals a glimpse of the villa through the trees which have, since Le Nôtre's original layout, matured to romantic grandeur. (Museum of Fine Arts, Boston)

Fig. 123—"A Flight of Steps Among Trees in the Park at Arcueil." Oudry discovered the run-down gardens of the Prince de Guise a few miles south of Paris in the early 1740s. Like Watteau, he was attracted to the romantic setting of nature running wild within the formal outlines of an old garden. (Cabinet des Dessins, Musée du Louvre)

Fig. 124—Method for laying out a formal terrace from the English translation of *La Theorie et la Pratique du Jardinage.* (Collection of the author)

Fig. 125—*"La Ferme."* By J. B. Oudry. (Photograph courtesy of Girardon, Musée du Louvre)

Fig. 126—*La villa d'Este.* By J.-H. Fragonard. (Orleans Musée des Beaux-Arts)

Fig. 127—*Le Moulin Joli.* By H. Robert. (Photograph courtesy of Girardon, *Musée Île de France*)

Fig. 128—*Project por le Jardin Anglo-Chinois du Petit Trianon.* Le Rouge reproduced Antoine Richard's plan in 1774. The formal parterres extend on three sides of the building in an uncertain transition into the informal landscape beyond. Like Palladio's Villa Rotunda, the little château's four perspectives provided an opportunity for a different landscape scene in each direction. (Dumbarton Oaks Garden Library)

Fig. 129—*Jardins de la Reine.* The informal grounds have in this plan by Richard Micque engulfed the little château. It was reproduced by Le Rouge in 1783. (Dumbarton Oaks Garden Library)

Fig. 130—Marie Antoinette's *Hameau* looking across the lake around 1900–1910. Hubert Robert participated in its planning and design. (Photograph by Eugene Atget, courtesy of Caisse Nationale des Monuments Historiques et des Sites.)

Fig. 131—Restored English park at *Rambouillet*. (Photograph courtesy Patrick Bracco)

Fig. 132—*Le Pavillon Chinois dans le Parc du Désert*. One of the finest eighteenth-century Chinese pavilions, it was allowed to disappear in the twentieth. (Collection of the author)

Fig. 133—*Plan du domaine de Moulin Joli à Colombes vers 1780*. (Archives Nationale)

Fig. 134—*Vue de Tente Tartare. Parc Monceau*. (Dumbarton Oaks Garden Library)

Fig. 135—*Vue de la hauteur du Minaret. Parc Monceau*. (Dumbarton Oaks Garden Library)

Fig. 136—*Coupe du nouveau Berceau ou Jardin D'Hiver. Parc Monceau*. Music room is above cave in structure at upper left. (Dumbarton Oaks Garden Library)

Fig. 137—*La Maison du Désert de M. de Monville*. The Column House is now (1978) being slowly restored. (Collection of the author)

Fig. 138—*Rocher vue de l'intérieur du Jardin Faisant Entrée du Désert par la Foret de Marly*. (Bibliothèque Nationale)

Fig. 139—Theater at the *Désert de Retz*. The stone face of the stage is half-buried in this old photograph. The Column House is to the left about 100 yards up the slope. (Collection of Olivier Chopin de Janvry)

Fig. 140—Theater of the *Désert* as engraved by Le Rouge. The basic setting is correct except for the missing Column House, which, in fact, could be seen instead of the romantic little cottage. The ornamental details are completely fanciful. See Fig. 139. (Dumbarton Oaks Garden Library)

Fig. 141—Theater project for *le Petit Trianon* by Richard Micque. (Dumbarton Oaks Garden Library)

Fig. 142—*Hôtel Thelusson*. View of arch from street, after 1780. (Cabinet des Estampes, Bibliothèque Nationale)

Fig. 143—*Moitié du Grand Treillage Meridional du Jardin de M. de la Bossiere*. From Le Rouge. (Dumbarton Oaks Garden Library)

Fig. 144—*Chaumière de Coquillage* at Rambouillet. (Photograph courtesy of Patrick Bracco)

Figs. 145-146—*Extérieur de la Chaumière du Jardin Anglais à M. le Comte d'Harcourt*. (Dumbarton Oaks Garden Library)

Fig. 147—*Jardins de Bagatelle*. Bagatelle, like many of the late eighteenth-century gardens, became a veritable botanical museum with extensive collections of trees and plants from all over the world. North American were particularly popular, and Thomas Jefferson supplied many of his friends in Paris with examples from Virginia. Gardeners like Thomas Blaikie were much in demand because of their horticultural experience. Both American and English botanical books were quickly translated. (Cabinet des Estampes, Bibliothèque Nationale)

Fig. 148—Grotto at the *Folie de Saint-James*. By. F.-J. Belanger. (Cabinet des Estampes, Bibliothèque Nationale)

Fig. 149—*Plan Général de la Maison Saint James à Neuilly*. By J.-F. Belanger. (Cabinet des Estampes, Bibliothèque Nationale)

Fig. 150—*Plan de la maison et du jardin de Beaumarchais*. Beaumarchais built his house and garden on a narrow strip of ground near the ancient *porte Saint-Antoine* in 1788. The architect of the house was Paul Lemoine, who worked with Belanger on the remarkable gardens. (Bibliothèque Historique de la Ville de Paris)

Fig. 151—*Vues de l'Hermitage* at *Ermenonville*. (Cabinet des Estampes, Bibliothèque Nationale)

Fig. 152—*Project de cabane en forme de temple primitif*. By A.-T. Brongniart. (Paris, Collection Particulaire. Photograph courtesy of the Caisse Nationale des Monuments Historiques et des Sites.)

Fig. 153—The Park at *Ermenonville*. By F. Mayer. (Reproduced from *La Gaz. Ill. des Amateurs de Jardins*, 1925. Collection of the author)

Fig. 154—General plan of *Méréville*. By Marin. (Reproduced from *La Gaz. Ill. des Amateurs de Jardins*, 1921. Collection of the author)

Fig. 155—*La Grande Cascade de Méréville*. (Collection of the author)

Fig. 156—The new grotto setting for Girardon's Apollo group at Versailles by H. Robert. Robert also worked on the *Hameau* for the Queen. (Photograph by the author)

Fig. 157—*Vue Général du Parc de Méréville.* (Collection of the author)

Fig. 158—*Le Parc de Méréville.* By H. Robert. The classical dairy can be seen beyond the bridge on the edge of the lake. (Photograph courtesy of Roger Viollet)

Fig. 159—View of column above Grand Cascade at *Méréville.* (Collection of the author)

Fig. 160—*Paysage avec Pont et Temple d'Amour.* By H. Robert. (Photograph courtesy of Roger Viollet)

Fig. 161—*Les Cascades de Tivoli.* By H. Robert. (Photograph courtesy of Girardon)

Fig. 162—*La Laiterie à Méréville.* (Collection of the author)

Fig. 163—*La Laiterie à Rambouillet.* The dairy was part of development of the park after it was acquired by Louis XVI. In 1785 the King established an experimental farm there. The dairy was designed by Thevenin and the decor was by Pierre Julien. (Cabinet des Estampes, Bibliothèque Nationale)

Fig. 164—Interior of dairy at Rambouillet. A similar figure was placed in the dairy at Méréville. (Photograph courtesy of Patrick Bracco)

Fig. 165—"View of Tivoli." By C.-J. Vernet. (Seattle Art Museum)

Fig. 166—*Grande Roche d'Après Vernet.* From Le Rouge. (Dumbarton Oaks Garden Library)

Fig. 167—*L' Île Natalie à Méréville.* (Collection of the author)

Fig. 168—*Vue Perspective du Pont de la Loüe.* By Ledoux. (Collection of the author)

Notes

Chapter I: *Learning From Paradise*

1. Forbes Sieveking, ed., *Sir William Temple Upon The Gardens of Epicurus* (London: 1908), p. 214.
2. George L. Hersey, *Alfonso II and the Artistic Renewal of Naples, 1485–1495* (New Haven: 1969), p. 59. Hersey's reconstruction of Alfonso's architecture is imaginative and useful. See also his "Poggioreale: Notes on a Reconstruction and an Early Replication," *Architectura*, Berlin, 1973. See also Terry Comito, *The Idea of the Garden in the Renaissance* (Rutgers: 1978).
3. Eugene Battisti, "Natura Artificiosa to Natura Artificialis," *Dumbarton Oaks Colloquium on the History of Landscape Architecture, I, The Italian Garden,* (Washington, D.C.: 1972), p. 14. See Professor Battisti's essay and that of Elisabeth MacDougall for valuable interpretations of the Rennaissance garden.
4. Ibid., p. 12.
5. Ibid., p. 13.
6. See generally Robert Harbison, *Eccentric Spaces* (New York: 1977), on the nostalgia of gardens.
7. Marie Gothein, *A History of Garden Art,* ed. by W. P. Wright, trans. by Mrs. Archer-Hind (London: 1928), vol. I, p. 393.
8. Pierre de Crescent, *Rustican de libeur des champs,* Bibliothèque de l'Arsenal, ms. 5064.
9. Translated from Italian into French and printed by I. Kenner (Paris: 1546).
10. Naomi Miller, *French Renaissance Fountains* (New York: 1977), p. 24. Professor Miller's dissertation, now available in the Garland Series of Outstanding Dissertations, is indispensable to any student of the art and architecture of the French Renaissance.
11. Ibid., quoted on p. 27. Summerson's essay can be found in *Heavenly Mansions* (New York: 1963), Chap. II, "Antithesis of the Quattrocento."
12. Ibid., pp. 25–31.
13. Ibid., p. 31.
14. E. Chirol, *Le Château de Gaillon: Un premier foyer de la Renaissance en France* (Rouen: 1952), has a full account of the château. Early records may be found in M. Rosci and A. Chastel, "Un château français en Italie. Un portrait de Gaillon à Gaglianico," *Art de France* III, Paris, 1963, pp. 103–113. Again, Miller is essential.
15. P. Lesueur, "Pacello de Mercogliano et les jardins d'Amboise, de Blois et de Gaillon," *Bulletin de la Société de l'Histoire de l'Art Français,* 1935 [1936], pp. 90–117.
16. Jacques Le Sieur, *Le Livre des fontaines de Rouen,* 1525. Quoted by Miller, p. 65.
17. Jacques Androet du Cerceau, *Le Premier volume des plus excellents bastiments de France* (Paris: 1576), p. 7.
18. Charles Seymour, Jr., *Michelangelo's David: A Search for Identity* (New York: 1974), p. 85. See also Howard Hibbard, *Michelangelo* (New York: 1974), pp. 52–53.

Chapter II: *Grottos, Water and Other Garden Fantasies*

1. On the development of the grotto see Miller, Chap. VII, "The Fountain in the Grotto," and also Lucile Golson, "Serlio, Primaticcio and the Architectural Grotto," *Gazette des Beaux-Arts,* XXVII, pp. 96–107.
2. Quoted in André Chastel, *The Crisis of the Renaissance* (Geneva: 1968), p. 43.
3. Ibid.
4. Henry Morley, *Palissey the Potter,* 2nd ed. London, p. 319. See also *A Delectable Garden,* trans. by H. Fox (1965).
5. Battisti, "Natura Artificiosa to Natura Artificialis," p. 30.
6. Eleanor Clark, *Hadrian's Villa,* rev. ed., (New York: 1974), p. 161.

7. Charles Moore, *Water and Architecture,* unpublished dissertation, Princeton University, 1957, p. 140.

8. Christopher Tunnard, "Adventure of Water," *Architectural Review* 86 (Sept. 1939), p. 101.

9. Philippe de Cossé Brissac, *Châteaux de France disparus* (Paris: 1947), p. 53.

10. Leon Battista Alberti, *Ten Books on Architecture,* English trans. by James Leoni (London: 1955), Book IX, Chap. IV, p. 192.

11. James Ackerman, *The Cortile Del Belvedere* (Vatican City: 1954), p. 45.

12. Quoted in Miller, *French Renaissance Fountains,* p. 100, from Vasari's *Life of Primaticcio.*

13. Frances Yates, *The Valois Tapestries,* 2nd ed. (London: 1975), p. 54. See Yates generally for a vivid account of the court entertainments as state policy in the sixteenth century.

14. Ibid., Introduction, p. XXIV.

Chapter III: *Premises of Order*

1. *Stressing Harmony*

1. Charles Éstienne, *Maison rustique, or the Countrie Farm,* trans. by Richard Surflet (London: 1600), p. 1.

2. For a full account of Philibert de l'Orme's work see A. Blunt, *Philibert de l'Orme* (London: 1958).

3. An excellent discussion of the iconography of Anet can be found in F. Bardon, *Diane de Poitiers et le mythe de Diane* (Paris: 1963).

4. Derek Clifford, *A History of Garden Design* (New York: 1963), p. 70.

5. Quoted in H. Inigo Triggs, *Garden Craft in Europe* (London: 1913), p. 74.

6. For a general account of Montceaux see Rosalys Coope, *Salomon de Brosse and the Development of the Classical Style in French Architecture from 1565 to 1630* (London: 1972), and also "The Château of Montceaux-en-Brie," *Journal of the Warburg and Courtauld Institutes* 22, 1-2 (1959), pp. 71–87. A Marie, in his *Jardins français Crées à la Renaissance* (Paris: 1955), accepts the primary role of Primaticcio.

7. L. Huygens, "Châteaux et jardins de l'Île de France d'après un journal de voyage de 1655," trans. by H. L. Brugmens, *Gazette des Beaux-Arts* Ser. 6, XVIII (Sept. 1937), p. 99.

8. H. de La Tourrasse, "Le Chateau-Neuf de Saint-Germain-en-Laye," *Gazette des Beaux-Arts* Ser. 5, IX (1924), p. 74.

9. Salomon de Caus, *Les Raisons des forces mouvantes avec diverses machines tant utilles que plaisantes,* (Frankfurt: 1615), Book 2. See also Christine Sondrina Maks, *Solomon de Caus 1576–1626* (Paris: 1935).

10. Hersey, *Alfonso II and Renewal of Naples,* pp. 87–88.

11. Quoted in Gothein, *History of Garden Art,* vol. I, p. 424.

12. Quoted in Franklin Hamilton Hazelhurst, *Jacques Boyceau and the French Formal Garden* (Athens: 1966), p. 23.

13. Gothein, *History of Garden Art,* vol. I, p. 418.

14. Quoted in Hazelhurst, *Jacques Boyceau,* p. 27.

15. See Hazelhurst, *Jacques Boyceau,* for excellent discussion on the importance of religion and philosophical ideas to seventeenth-century garden theories, particularly pp. 28–29.

16. Ibid., p. 32.

17. Ibid., p. 33

18. Ibid., p. 38.

19. Ibid., p. 45.

20. See Sten Karling, "The Importance of André Mollet and His Family for the Development of the French Formal Garden," *Dumbarton Oaks Colloquium on the History of Landscape Architecture, III, The French Formal Garden* (Washington, D.C.: 1974), pp. 17-25 for a good discussion on *Le Jardin de plaisir.*

21. André Mollet, *The Garden of Pleasure* (London: 1670), Preface.

22. William P. Stern, "Masters Memorial Lecture," *Journal of the Royal Horticultural Society* (August 1965), p. 322.

23. Triggs, *Garden Craft,* p. 39.

24. Ibid., pp. 38–39.

25. Georgina Masson, "Italian Flower Collectors' Gardens," *The Italian Garden* (Washington, D.C.: 1972), p. 66.

26. Ibid., p. 66.

Chapter III: *Premises of Order*

2. *Sweete Retirements*

27. Sieveking, *William Temple Upon Gardens,* pp. 208–220. All of the quotations of John Evelyn are taken from this edition.

28. See Professor Hazelhurst's chapter, "The Theory in Fact," in *Jacques Boyceau,* for a detailed account of the creation of the Luxembourg. Also Runor Strandberg, "Jacques Boyceau, His Theory of Landscape Gardening and Some of His Creations," *Konsthistorisk tidskrift* 37 (1968).

29. See Alfred Cremail, *Le Château de Rueil et ses jardins sous le Cardinal de Richelieu* (Paris: 1888), for general account of Rueil.

30. Sieveking, *William Temple Upon Gardens,* p. 208.

31. For a full study and interpretation of the problems of the Cascade de Saint-Cloud, see Robert W. Berger, *Antoine Le Pautre, A French Architect of the Era of Louis XIV* (New York: 1969), pp. 47–64. Plan with cascade and Maison de Gondi, Bibliothèque Nationale, Cabinet des Estampes, Va. 488a.

Chapter III: *Premises of Order*

3. *Garden as Theater*

32. George R. Kernodle, *From Art to Theatre: Form and Convention in the Renaissance* (Chicago: 1944), p. 174.
33. Ackerman, p. 19. Also see Arnaldo Bruschi, *Bramante* (London: 1974), pp. 87–114.
34. T.E. Lawrence, *The French Stage in the XVII Century* (Manchester: 1957), pp. 127–128.
35. Sieveking, *William Temple Upon Gardens*, p. 208.
36. Ibid., p. 211.
37. Ibid., p. 211.
38. Battisti, "*Natura Artificiosa* to *Natura Artificialis*," p. 14.
39. The word "perspective" in the seventeenth century was the term normally used for a painted backdrop. Silvestre's engraving correctly identified the Arc de Triomphe at Rueil as "La Perspective."
40. Quoted by Dora Wiebenson in her study, *The Picturesque Garden in France* (Princeton: 1978), pp. 97–98.

Chapter IV: *Labors in Perfection*

1. *Le Nôtre*

1. F. Gentil, *Le Jardinier solitaire* (Paris: 1704), p. 1.
2. Jules Guiffrey, "Liste des Artistes et Artisans," *Bulletin de la Société de l'Histoire de l'Art Français* (1872), p. 35.
3. The earliest description of the Château de Richelieu is in E. Brackenhoffer, *Voyage en France, 1643–1644*. See also Reginald Blomfield, *A History of French Architecture From the Reign of Charles VIII till the Death of Mazarin* (London: 1911), Vol. 2, p. 61.
4. Allan Graham and Peter Smith, *François Mansart* (London: 1973), p. 103. See also "La vie de Jules Hardouin Mansart," an unpublished manuscript in the Bibliothèque Nationale, ms. NA. Fr. 22936 noting that "M. Mansart . . . has contributed not a little by his teaching and his lessons, great architect as he was, to provide openings to the said Sr. le Nôtre . . ."

Chapter IV: *Labors in Perfection*

2. *Versailles*

5. Blomfield, *History of French Architecture*, vol. II, p. 141.
6. Quoted in Hazelhurst, *Jacques Boyceau*, p. 68.
7. Fouquet's own copy with his own ambitious squirrel embossed on the cover is now in the Garden Library of Dumbarton Oaks, Washington.
8. Any serious study of Vaux-le-Vicomte must begin with a thorough investigation of the restored gardens armed with Silvestre's contemporary plan and views. Only then can the inadequate literature be understood. For a basic account of the gardens one should begin with Louis Hautecoeur, *Histoire de l'architecture classique en France* vol. II (Paris: 1948), pp. 379–382. Mlle. de Scudery, Fountaine, and even Anatole France are all worth reading as a background to Fouquet and his Parnassus. W.H. Ward, *The Architecture of the Renaissance in France* (London: 1911), vol. II, has a brief account of the château. The plates reproduced in E. de Ganay, *André Le Nostre, 1613–1700* (Paris: 1962), are good.
9. André Félibien, *Fête de Versailles en 1678* (Paris: 1678).
10. *Letters of Madame de Sévigné, Selected and Translated by Violet Hammersley* (London: 1955), p. 167.
11. The central group of sculpture is the celebrated work by François Girardon. It was moved several times after the grotto was destroyed and was finally placed in Hubert Robert's rustic installation. See also Liliane Lange, "La Grotte de Thétis et le premier Versailles de Louis XIV," *Art de France* I, (Paris, 1961), pp. 133–148.
12. André Félibien, *Description sommière du Château de Versailles* (Paris: 1674).
13. The best study of Montmorency is H. Junecke, *Montmorency* (Berlin: 1960). See also *Watteau et son école* (Paris: 1924). Silvestre made three engravings of Montmorency and a plan of the gardens was made by Mariette, vol. II, Plate 345. Silvestre's drawings are in the Louvre.
14. F. Hamilton Hazelhurst, "Le Nostre at Conflans, Garden of the Archbishop of Paris," *The French Formal Garden*, pp. 29–40.
15. *Saint-Simone at Versailles*, trans. by Lucy Norton (London: 1958), p. 265.
16. Ganay, *Andre Le Nostre*, p. 131.

Chapter V: *After Le Nôtre: A Sentimental Journey*

1. Richard Fargher, *Life and Letters in France, II, The Eighteenth Century* (London: 1970), p. XIV.
2. The programmed visit or promenade of French gardens was a well-developed ritual by the late sixteenth century. Even during the *Directoire*, the public followed definite patterns of walking in the Tuileries according to the season. (See O. Choppin de Janvry, "Les Jardins Promenades au XVIII siècle," *Revue de Monuments Historiques de la France* 5 (1976), pp. 7–15. The text of the King's "Manière de montrer les jardins de Versailles," with an introduction by R.

Girardet, was published by Les Îles D'Or (Paris: 1951).

3. Jules Guiffrey, *Compte des bâtiments,* vols. 4–5.

4. Gilbert W. Barker, *Antoine Watteau* (London: 1939), p. 40. Quotes the Comte de Caylus, "ce fut encore la qu'il dessinoit sans cesse les arbes de ce beau jardin, qui brut et moins peigne que ceux des autres maisons roiales, lui fournissat des points de vue infinis."

5. Pierre Daniel Huet, *Huetiana* (Paris: 1722). Quoted in Sieveking, *William Temple Upon Gardens,* p. 122.

6. Sieveking, *William Temple Upon Gardens,* p. 117.

7. The literature on the subject is voluminous, but see C. Hussey, *The Picturesque* (London: 1927) and later editions; also E. Mainwaring, *Italian Landscape in 18th Century England* (1925).

8. Geoffroy Atkinson and Abraham C. Keller, *Prelude to the Enlightenment,* quoting Prevost, *Memoirs d'un homme de qualité,* liv. 15 in *Oeuvres,* III, p. 184.

9. Hazelhurst, *Jacques Boyceau,* p. 32.

10. Ibid., p. 34.

11. Sieveking, *William Temple Upon Gardens,* p. 117.

12. Quoted in S. Lang, "Genesis of the Landscape Garden," *The Picturesque Garden and its Influence Outside the British Isles,* (Dumbarton Oaks, Washington: 1974), p. 14.

13. Ibid., p. 16.

14. Roger de Piles, *The Principles of Painting* (London: 1743), reprinted in *Literary Sources of Art History,* ed. by E. Holt (Princeton: 1947), pp. 406–407.

15. *French Landscape Drawings and Sketches of the Eighteenth Century* Catalogue (London: British Museum Publications, 1977), Introduction, p. 9.

16. Young, *Travels in France,* p. 11.

17. Ibid., p. 86.

18. Oswald Sirén, *China and the Gardens of Europe* (New York: 1950), p. 102.

19. *Gazette littérraire* (1771), VI, p. 369. Quoted in A. Lovejoy, *Essays in the History of Ideas* (Baltimore: 1948), p. 117.

20. Anthony Vidler, "The Architecture of the Lodges: Ritual Form and Associa-tional Life in the Late Enlightenment," *Oppositions* (Summer, 1976), p. 87.

21. *The Letters of Horace Walpole,* ed. by Mrs. Paget Toynbee (Oxford: 1904), Vol. IX, p. 241.

22. Thomas Whately, *Observations on Modern Gardening* (London: 1770), p. 64.

23. Sirén, *China and Gardens,* quoted p. 121.

24. *Jardins en France 1760–1820,* Catalogue of the 1977 exhibition of the Caisse Nationale des Monuments Historiques et des Sites prepared by C. Malecot and M. Mosser. This catalogue is a detailed survey of the subject both in text and illustration. Mme. Genlis's description is on p. 89, where there is an extensive treatment of the Désert de Retz.

25. Marcel Mayer, *Nicolas Michot* (Paris: 1942), pp. 12–14.

26. Thomas Blaikie, *Diary of a Scotch Gardener* (London: 1931), p. 154.

27. Horace Walpole, *On Modern Gardening* (London: 1975), p. 8.

28. Blaikie, *Diary of a Gardener,* p. 132.

29. Daniel Malthus was the father of Thomas Malthus, population theorist of the eighteenth century. He was a friend and student of Rousseau and helped the French philosopher settle in England.

30. Abbé J.B. Le Blanc, *Letters on the French and English Nations* (London: 1747), Vol. 3, p. 297.

31. Lang, *Genesis of Landscape Garden,* p. 36.

32. Blaikie, *Diary of a Gardener,* p. 154.

33. R. L. de Girardin, *De la composition des paysages, ou des moyens d'embellir la nature autour des habitations, en joignant l'agreable à l'utile* (Geneva: 1777), tr. by D. Malthus, London, 1783, p. 40.

34. Sirén, *China and Gardens,* p. 130.

35. Quoted in Sirén, *China and Gardens,* p. 154, from Bachaumont's *Mémoires secrets,* Vol. XXXI.

36. Stern, *Belanger,* (Paris: 19   ), pp. 29–30.

37. A. Bartlett Giamatti, *The Earthly Paradise and the Renaissance Epic* (Princeton: 1969), pp. 356–360. Professor Giamatti's study is very important to any student of garden history as it relates to the literary tradition.

A Selected Bibliography

In addition to the books and articles cited in the notes, the following works are provided not only to indicate the basic published sources used, but as an aid to the reader in following up hints within the text which could not be developed. Three hundred years represents a long span of French garden history and it is a subject that is interwoven with a number of other fields. Fireworks and botany, along with theater and politics are a part of that history. These topics, too extensive for this compilation, can nevertheless be pursued with profit.

The evolution of the French garden was, of course, intimately related to Renaissance architecture and architectural theory. Portions of that vast bibliography could easily be annexed to the list below.

Several recent studies in English have appeared and are indispensable works for anyone interested in the subject. These include *The French Formal Garden,* papers from the Dumbarton Oaks Colloquium on the History of Landscape Architecture, Hamilton Hazelhurst's study of Jacques Boyceau, Naomi Miller's *French Renaissance Fountains,* and Dora Weibenson's *The Picturesque Garden in France.* The exhibition held at the Hôtel de Sully in 1977 and the well-illustrated catalogue prepared by Claude Malecot and her colleagues are a useful contribution to the study of the French garden in the late eighteenth and early nineteenth centuries.

Ackerman, James S. *The Cortile Del Belevedere.* Vatican City: 1954.
Addison, J. "The Pleasures of the Imagination," *The Spectator* 411–422, 21 June–4 July, 1712.
Alberti, Leon Battista. *Ten Books on Architecture by Leon Battista Alberti.* Italian translation Cosimo Bartoli; English translation James Leoni; ed. Rykwert. London: 1955.
Androuet, du Cerceau, J. *Le Premier (Second) Volume des plus excellents bastiments de France.* 2 vols. Paris: 1576–1579.
——————. *Second Livre d'architecture.* Paris: 1561.
Attiret, J. D. *A Particular Account of the Emperor of China's Gardens Near Pekin.* Trans. Sir. H. Beaumont. London: 1752.

Barbet, L. A. *Les Grandes Eaux de Versailles.* Paris: 1907.
Bardon, F. *Diane de Poitiers et le mythe de Diane.* Paris: 1963.
Batiffol, L. "Le château de Versailles de Louis XIII et son architecture Philibert Le Roy." *Gazette des Beaux-Arts.* Ser. 4, X, Nov. 1913, pp. 341–371.
Berger, Robert W. *Antoine Le Pautre, A French Architect of the Era of Louis XIV.* New York: 1969.
Berluchon, L. *Jardins de Touraine.* Tours: 1940.
Blaikie, T. *Diary of a Scotch Gardener at the French Court at the End of the Eighteenth Century.* Ed. F. Birrell. London: 1931.
Blomfield, R. T. *A History of French Architecture from the Reign of Charles VIII till the Death of Mazarin.* 2. Vols. London: 1911.
Blondel, Jacques François. *Architecture françoise.* 4 vols. Paris: 1752–1756.
——————. *De la distribution des maisons de plaisance et de la décoration des edifices en général.* Paris: 1937. Reprinted, 2 vols. Farnborough: 1967.
Blunt, A. *Art and Architecture in France, 1500–1700.* 2nd ed. Harmondsworth, Baltimore: 1957.
——————. *Philibert de l'Orme.* London: 1958.
Boucher, F. "Les Jardins des Tuileries & du Luxembourg." *Gazette illustrée des amateurs de jardins* 1940–1947, pp. 10–17.
Bouillet, A. *La Folie de Sainte-James à Neuilly.* Paris: 1894.
Boyceau, J. *Traité du jardinage selon les raisons de la nature et de l'art.* Ed. J. de Menours. Paris: 1638.

Bracco, P. *Feu d'Artifice*. Washington: 1976

Bus, C. du, "Le Plus Ancien Plan de Versailles." *Gazette des Beaux-Arts*. Ser. 5, XIV, Sept.–Oct. 1926, pp. 183–197.

Carrogis, L. (known as Carmontelle). *Jardin de Monçeau, près de Paris*. Paris: 1779.

Caus, I. de. *Nouvelles inventions de lever l'eau plus hault que sa source*. London: 1644.

Caus, S. de. *Les Raisons des forces Mouvantes avec diverses machines tant utilles que plaisantes*. Frankfurt: 1615.

Cayeux, J. de. "Hubert Robert dessinateur des jardins et sa collaboration au Parc de Méréville." *Bulletin de la Société de l'Histoire de l'Art Français*. 1968.

Chambers, William. *A Dissertation on Oriental Gardening*. London: 1772.

Charageat, M. *L'Art des jardins*. Paris: 1962.

——————. "La Nymphée de Wideville et la grotte du Luxembourg." *Bulletin de la Société de l'Histoire de l'Art Français*. 1934.

Chase, Isabel W. U. *Horace Walpole: Gardenist*. Princeton: 1943.

Chirol, E. *Le Château de Gaillon. Un premier foyer de la Renaissance en France*. Rouen: 1952.

Choppin de Janvry, O. "Avant que disparaisse à jamais de Désert de Retz." *L'Oeil* 151–152, Sept. 1967, pp. 30–41.

——————. "Méréville." *L'Oeil* 182, Dec. 1969, pp. 30–41.

Clifford, D. P. *A History of Garden Design*. New York: 1963.

Coffin, D. R. *The Villa d'Este at Tivoli*. Princeton: 1960.

Colonna, Francesco, *Hypnerotomachia Poliphili*. Critical edition and commentary by G. Pozzi and L. A. Ciapponi, 2 vols. Padua: 1964.

R. Coope. "The Chateau of Montceaux-en-Brie." *Journal of the Warburg and Courtauld Institutes* 22, 1–2, 1959, pp. 71–87.

——————. *Salomon de Brosse and the Development of the Classical Style in French Architecture from 1565 to 1630*. London: 1972.

Corpechot, L. *Les Jardins de l'intelligence*. Paris: 1912.

Cosse Brissac, P. de. *Châteaux de France disparus*. Paris: 1947.

Crémail, A. *Le Château de Rueil et ses jardins sous le Cardinal de Richelieu*. Paris: 1888.

Crisp, Frank. *Medieval Gardens*. Ed. C. C. Paterson, 2 vols. London: 1924.

Crump, P. E. *Nature in the Age of Louis XIV*. London: 1928.

Dan, P. *Le Tresor des Merveilles de la maison royale de Fontainebleau*. Paris: 1642.

Delille, J. *Les Jardins, ou l'art d'embellir les paysages, Poeme*. Paris: 1782.

Desjardins, G. A. *Le Petit-Trianon, Histoire et description*. Versailles: 1885.

Dezallier d'Argenville, Antoine Joseph. *La Théorie et la Pratique du jardinage*. Paris: 1709.

Dezallier d'Argenville, Antoine Nicolas. *Voyage Pittoresque des environs de Paris*. Third edition. Paris: 1768.

Dimier, L. "Bernard Palissy, rocailleur, fontenier et decorateur de jardins." *Gazette des Beaux-Arts*. Ser. 6, XII, July 1934, pp. 8–29.

Encyclopedia of World Art. 14 vols. New York: 1959–1967.

Éstienne, C. and Liébault, J. *Maison rustique, or The Countrie Farme*. Trans. R. Surfet London: 1600.

Evelyn, J. *Diary, 1641–1705/6*. London: 1906.

Fargher, R. *Life and Letters in France, II, The Eighteenth Century*. London: 1970.

Félibien Des Avaux, A. *Description de la grotte de Versailles*. Paris: 1679.

Fons Sapentiae: Garden Fountains in Illustrated Books, Sixteenth–Eighteenth Centuries. Catalogue by E. B. MacDougall, N. Miller, L. Byers. Washington, D.C.: 1977.

French Landscape Drawings and Sketches of the Eighteenth Century. Catalogue, British Museum. London: 1977.

Gadol, J. *Leon Battista Alberti: Universal Man of the Early Renaissance*. Chicago: 1969.

Ganay, E. de, *André Le Nostre, 1613–1700*. Paris: 1962.

——————. "Le Jardin d'Ermenonville," *Gazette illustrée des amateurs de jardins*. 1925.

——————. *Les Jardins de France et leur décor*. Paris: 1949.

Gebelin, F. *Les Châteaux de la Renaissance*. Paris: 1927.

Gentil, F. *Le Jardinier solitaire*. Paris: 1704.

Giamatti, A. B. *The Earthly Paradise and the Renaissance Epic*. Princeton: 1966.

Gibault, G. *Les Anciens Jardins de Fontainebleau*. Paris: 1913.

Girardin, R. L. de. *An Essay on Landscape*. Trans. D. Malthus. London: 1783.

——————. *De la composition des paysages, ou Des moyens d'embellir la nature autour des habitations, en joignant l'agréable à l'utile*. Geneva-Paris: 1777.

Gothein, M. L. *A History of Garden Art*. Ed. W. P. Wright, trans. Mrs. Archer-Hind, 2 vols. London-Toronto: 1928.

Graham, A. and Smith, P. *François Mansart*. London: 1973.

Gromort, G. *Le Hameau de Trianon, Histoire et description*. Paris: 1928.

Guiffrey, J. M. J. *André Le Nostre*. Paris: 1912.

—————. *Comptes des Bâtiments du roi sous le règne de Louis XIV.* 5 vols. Paris: 1881–1901.

Harbison, R. *Eccentric Spaces*. New York: 1977.

Hautecoeur, L. *Histoire de l'architecture classique en France.* 4 vols. Paris: 1943–1957.

—————. *Les Jardins des dieux et des hommes*. Paris: 1959.

Hazelhurst, F. *Jacques Boyceau and the French Formal Garden*. Athens, Ga.: 1966.

—————. "Le Nostre at Conflans, Garden of the Archbishop of Paris," Dumbarton Oaks Colloquium on the History of Landscape Architecture, III. *The French Formal Garden.* Washington, D.C.: 1974, pp. 27–40.

Hermann, Wolfgang. *Laugier and Eighteenth Century French Theory.* London: 1962.

Hersey, G. *Alfonso II and the Artistic Renewal of Naples 1485–1495.* New Haven: 1969.

Hirshfeld, C. C. L. *Théorie de l'art des jardins.* 5 vols. Leipzig: 1779–1785.

Hygens, L. "Châteaux et jardins de l'Île de France d'après un journal de voyage de 1655." Trans. H. L. Brugmans, *Gazette des Beaux-Arts.* Ser. 6, XVIII, Sept. 1937, pp. 93–114.

Jacquot, J., ed. *Les Fêtes de la Renaissance.* Paris: 1956.

Jardins en France, 1760–1820. Catalogue, Caisse Nationale de Monuments Historiques et des Sites. Paris: 1977.

Jellicoe, S. and G. *Water: The Use of Water in Landscape Architecture.* London: 1971.

Junecke, H. *Montmorency.* Berlin: 1960.

Kerling, Sten. "The Importance of André Mollet and his Family for the Development of the French Formal Garden," Dumbarton Oaks Colloquium on the History on Landscape Architecture, III. *The French Formal Garden.* Washington, D.C.: 1974. pp. 1–26.

Kernodle, G. R. *From Art to Theater, Form and Convention in the Renaissance.* Chicago: 1944.

Kimball, S. F. *The Creation of the Rococo.* Philadelphia: 1943.

Laborde, A. L. J. de. *Descriptions des nouveaux jardins de la France, et ses anciens châteaux, Paris.* 1808–1825.

Laborde, L. E. S. J. de. *Les Comptes des bâtiments du roi (1528–1571).* Ed. J. Guiffrey, 2 vols. Paris: 1877–1880.

Lange, L. "La grotte de Thétis et la premier Versailles de Louis XIV." *Art de France* I, Paris, 1961, pp. 133–148.

Lawrence, T. E. *The French Stage in the XVIII Century.* Manchester: 1957.

Le Brun, Charles. *Recueil de desseins de fontaines et de frises maritimes.* Paris: 1693(?)

Le Camus de Mezieres, Nicholas (?) *Description des eaux de Chantilly et de Hameau.* Paris: 1783.

Lefevre, J. "Méréville." *Gazette illustrée des amateurs de jardins.* 1921.

Le Pautre, J. *Grottes et veues de jardins.* Paris: n. d.

Le Rouge, G. L. *Cahiers de jardins anglo-chinois.* Paris: 1776–1785.

Lesueur, F. *Le Château d'Amboise.* Paris: 1935.

—————— and P. *Le Château de Blois.* Paris: 1921.

Lesueur, P. *Les Jardins du Château de Blois et leurs dependances.* Blois: 1904–1905.

—————— and F. "Pacello de Mercogliano et les jardins d'Amboise, de Vlois et de Gaillon." *Bulletin de la Société de l'Histoire de l'Art Français.* 1936.

Lesueur, P. "Fra Giocondo en France." *Bulletin de la Société de l'Histoire de l'art de France,* 1931, pp. 115–144.

Lister, M. *A Journey to Paris in the Year 1698.* London: 1699.

Louis XIV. *Manière de montrer les jardins de Versailles,* with intro. by R. Girardet. Paris: 1951.

MacDougall, E. "Ars Hortulorum: Sixteenth Century Garden Iconography and Literary Theory in Italy," Dumbarton Oaks Colloquium on the History of Landscape Architecture, I. *The Italian Garden.* Washington, D.C.: 1972, pp. 37–60.

Marot, J. *Le Magnifique Chasteau de Richelieu.* Paris: 1670.

Masson, G. *Italian Gardens.* London: 1959.

Marie, Alfred. *Jardins Français Crées à la Renaissance.* Paris: 1955.

—————. *Naissance de Versailles, le château, les jardins.* 2 vols. Paris: 1968.

Marot, J. *L'Architecture française.* Paris: 1670. Reprinted as vol. 4 of Mariette's *Architecture française.* Paris: 1970.

Mayer, M. *Le Château d'Anet.* Paris: 1961.

McDougall, Dorothy. *Two Royal Domains of France. The Tuileries and Versailles in Garden History, Art, and Anecdote.* London: 1931.

Mefanes, J. "A Spontaneous Feeling for Nature." *Apollo* 104, Nov. 1976.

Merian, M. *Topographia Galliae.* Amsterdam: 1660. Reprinted Paris.

Miller, N. *French Renaissance Fountains.* New York: 1977.

Mollet, A. *Le Jardin de plaisirs.* Stockholm: 1651.

Mollet, C. *Théâtre des plans et jardinages.* Paris: 1652.

Moore, C. "Water and Architecture," unpublished dissertation. Princeton University: 1957.

Mousset, A. *Les Francine, créateurs des eaux de Versailles.* Paris: 1930.

Nolhac, A. M. P. G. de. *La Création de Versailles, Étude sur les origines et les premières trans-formations du château et des jardins*. Versailles: 1901.
_____. *Les Jardins de Versailles*. Paris: 1906.

Palissy, B. *The Admirable Discourses of Bernard Palissy*. 1580. Trans. A. La Rocque. Urbana: 1952.
Perelle, A. *Les places, portes, fontaines, eglises, et maisons de Paris*. Paris: n. d.
_____. *Les Plans, profils, et elévations des villes*. Paris: 1714–1715.
_____. *Recueil général du château de Versailles*. Paris: 1664–1689.
_____. *Veues des belles maisons de France*. Paris: n. d.
Piles, R. de. *The Principles of Painting*. London: 1743.
Poëte, M. *Au jardin des Tuileries, L'Art du jardin, La Promenade publique*. Paris: 1924.

Rosci, M. and Chastel, A. "Un château français en Italie. Un portrait de Gaillon à Gaglianico." *Art de France* III, Paris: 1963, pp. 103–113.
Ryckwert, J. *On Adam's House in Paradise*. New York: 1972.

Saint-Simon, Louis de Rouvroy. *Historical Memoires*. Ed. and trans. L. Norton, 2 vols. London: 1967.
Serlio, S. *Tutte l'Opere d'architettura, et prospectiva* [sic]. Ed. G. D. Scamozzi. Venice: 1660.
Serres, O de. *Le Théâtre d'Agriculture et mesnage des champs, Geneva*. 1651.
Sévigné, M. de. *Letters from Madame la Marquise de Sévigné*. Selected trans. and intro. by Violet Hammersley; preface by W. Somerset Maugham. London: 1955.
Seznec, J. *The Survival of the Pagan Gods*. New York: 1953.
Shearman, J. K. G. *Mannerism*. Harmondsworth: 1967.
Sieveking, A. F. *Sir William Temple Upon the Gardens of Epicurus*. London: 1908.
Silvestre, I. *Views of the gardens at Ruel with Grottos, Cascades, and Fountains*. n. d.
Sirén, O. *China and Gardens of Europe of the Eighteenth Century*. Trans. D. Burton. New York: 1950.
Stein, H. *Les Jardins de France*. Paris: 1913.
Stern, Jean. *À l'ombre de Sophie Arnould. François-Joseph Balanger, architecte des Menus Plaisirs*. 2 vols. Paris: 1930.
Stern, W. "Master Memorial Lecture." *Journal of the Royal Horticultural Society*, August, 1965.
Strandberg, R. "Jacques Boyceau, His Theory of Landscape Gardening and Some of His Creations." *Konsthistorisk tidskrift* 37, 1968.
Strong, Roy C. *Splendour at Court: Renaissance Spectacle and the Theater of Power*. New York: 1973.

Tilley, A. A. *The Dawn of the French Renaissance*. Cambridge: 1918.
Tourrasse, H. de la, "La Château-Neuf de Saint-Germain-en-Laye." *Gazette des Beaux-Arts*. Ser. 5, IX, 1924, pp. 68–89.
Triggs, H. I. *Garden Craft in Europe*. London: 1913.
Tunnard, C. "Adventure of Water." *Architectural Review* 86, Sept. 1939, pp. 99–102.

Vidler, A., "The Architecture of Lodges. Ritual Form and Associational Life in the Late Enlightenment." *Oppositions*, Summer, 1976.

Ward, William Henry. *The Architecture of the Renaissance in France*. 2 vols. London: 1911.
_____. *French Châteaux and Gardens in the XVIth Century*. London: 1909.
Watelet, C. H. *Essai sur les jardins*. Paris: 1774.
Weiss, R. "The Castle of Gaillon in 1509–10." *Journal of the Warburg and Courtauld Institutes* 16–12, 1953, pp. 1–12.
Wiebenson, D. *The Picturesque Garden in France*. Princeton: 1978.
Whately, T. *Observations on Modern Gardening*. London: 1770.

Yates, F. A. *The French Academies of the Sixteenth Century*. London: 1947.
_____. *The Valois Tapestries*. 2nd edition. London: 1975.
Young, Arthur. *Travels during the Years 1787, 1788, and 1789*. 2 vols. Bury St. Edmunds: 1792–1794.

Zerner, H. *The School of Fontainebleau: Etchings and Engravings*. Trans. S. Brown. New York: 1969.

Index

Sources of Illustrations

The author and publisher would like to thank each individual and institution for permission to publish the material listed below.

Front cover: Musée de Versailles, Clichés Musées Nationaux, Paris.
Frontispiece: Bibliothèque École des Beaux Arts, Paris. Photographie Giraudon, Paris.
Back cover: Archives Nationales, Paris.

1.—British Museum, London.
2.—Dumbarton Oaks Research Library and Collections, Washington, D.C.
3.—British Museum, London.
4.—Dumbarton Oaks Research Library and Collections, Washington, D.C.
5.—Dumbarton Oaks Research Library and Collections, Washington, D.C.
6.—British Museum, London.
7.—Dumbarton Oaks Research Library and Collections, Washington, D.C.
8.—Dumbarton Oaks Research Library and Collections, Washington, D.C.
9.—Cabinet d'Estampes, Bibliothèque Nationale, Paris.
10.—Dumbarton Oaks Research Library and Collections, Washington, D.C.
11.—Dumbarton Oaks Research Library and Collections, Washington, D.C.
12.—Cabinet d'Estampes, Bibliothèque Nationale, Paris.
13.—Louvre, Cabinet des Dessins, Documentation Photographique de la Réunion des Musées Nationaux, Paris.
14.—Alfred Marie, *Le Jardin Français.*
15.—Dumbarton Oaks Research Library and Collections, Washington, D.C.
16.—Dumbarton Oaks Research Library and Collections, Washington, D.C.
17.—Dumbarton Oaks Research Library and Collections, Washington, D.C.
18.—Cabinet d'Estampes, Bibliothèque Nationale, Paris.
19.—Dumbarton Oaks Research Library and Collections, Washington, D.C.
20.—Courtauld Institute of Art, London.
21.—Courtauld Institute of Art, London.
22.—Courtauld Institute of Art, London.
23.—Dumbarton Oaks Research Library and Collections, Washington, D.C.
24.—Courtauld Institute of Art, London.
25.—Dumbarton Oaks Research Library and Collections, Washington, D.C.
26.—Dumbarton Oaks Research Library and Collections, Washington, D.C.
27.—National Gallery of Scotland, Edinburgh.
28.—Fogg Art Museum, Harvard University, Cambridge, Massachusetts.
29.—Courtauld Institute of Art, London.
30.—Cabinet d'Estampes, Bibliothèque Nationale, Paris.
31.—Photograph by author.
32.—British Museum, London.
33.—Cabinet d'Estampes, Bibliothèque Nationale, Paris.
34.—British Museum, London.
35.—Metropolitan Museum of Art, New York.
36.—Metropolitan Museum of Art, New York.
37.—British Museum, London.
38.—Collection of author.
39.—Photograph by author.
40.—Photograph by author.
41.—Cabinet d'Estampes, Bibliothèque Nationale, Paris.
42.—Cabinet d'Estampes, Bibliothèque Nationale, Paris.
43.—Cabinet d'Estampes, Bibliothèque Nationale, Paris.
44.—Cabinet d'Estampes, Bibliothèque Nationale, Paris.
45.—Alfred Marie, *Le Jardin Français.*
46.—Alfred Marie, *Le Jardin Français.*
47.—Photograph by author.

48.—Cabinet d'Estampes, Bibliothèque Nationale, Paris.
49.—Dumbarton Oaks Research Library and Collections, Washington, D.C.
50.—Dumbarton Oaks Research Library and Collections, Washington, D.C.
51.—Royal Library, Stockholm.
52.—Cabinet d'Estampes, Bibliothèque Nationale, Paris.
53.—Cabinet d'Estampes, Bibliothèque Nationale, Paris.
54.—Collection of author.
55.—Dumbarton Oaks Research Library and Collections, Washington, D.C.
56.—Collection of author.
57.—Collection of author.
58.—Cabinet d'Estampes, Bibliothèque Nationale, Paris.
59.—Cabinet d'Estampes, Bibliothèque Nationale, Paris.
60.—Collection of author.
61.—Caisse Nationale Monuments Historiques et des Sites, ATGET/c. Arch. Phot. Paris/ S.P.A.D.E.M.
62.—Caisse Nationale Monuments Historique et des Sites, ATGET/c. Arch. Phot. Paris/ S.P.A.D.E.M.
63.—Cabinet d'Estampes, Bibliothèque Nationale, Paris.
64.—Arnoldo Braschi, *Bramonte,* Thames & Hudson, 1977, London.
65.—Collection of author.
66.—Dumbarton Oaks Research Library and Collections, Washington, D.C.
67.—Cabinet d'Estampes, Bibliothèque Nationale, Paris.
68.—Metropolitan Museum of Art, New York.
69.—Metropolitan Museum of Art, New York.
70.—Metropolitan Museum of Art, New York.
71.—Metropolitan Museum of Art, New York.
72.—Metropolitan Museum of Art, New York.
73.—Cabinet d'Estampes, Bibliothèque Nationale, Paris.
74.—Cabinet d'Estampes, Bibliothèque Nationale, Paris.
75.—Dumbarton Oaks Research Library and Collections, Washington, D.C.
76.—Dumbarton Oaks Research Library and Collections, Washington, D.C.
77.—Cabinet d'Estampes, Bibliothèque Nationale, Paris.
78.—Dumbarton Oaks Research Library and Collections, Washington, D.C.
79.—Cabinet d'Estampes, Bibliothèque Nationale, Paris.
80.—Cabinet d'Estampes, Bibliothèque Nationale, Paris.
81.—Cabinet d'Estampes, Bibliothèque Nationale, Paris.
82.—Collection of author.
83.—Caisse Nationale des Monuments Historiques et des Sites, Arch. Phot. Paris.
84.—Cabinet d'Estampes, Bibliothèque Nationale, Paris.
85.—H. Roger-Viollet, Paris.
86.—Cabinet d'Estampes, Bibliothèque Nationale, Paris.
87.—Cabinet d'Estampes, Bibliothèque Nationale, Paris.
88.—Cabinet d'Estampes, Bibliothèque Nationale, Paris.
89.—Louvre, Cabinet des Dessins, Documentation Photographique de la Réunion des Musées Nationaux, Cliche des Musées Nationaux, Paris.
90.—Cabinet d'Estampes, Bibliothèque Nationale, Paris.
91.—Cabinet d'Estampes, Bibliothèque Nationale, Paris.
92.—Louvre, Cabinet des Dessins, Documentation Photographique de la Réunion des Musées Nationaux, Paris.
93.—Collection of author.
94.—Louvre, Cabinet des Dessins, Documentation Photographique de la Réunion des Musées Nationaux, Paris.
95.—Dumbarton Oaks Research Library and Collections, Washington, D.C.
96.—Dumbarton Oaks Research Library and Collections, Washington, D.C.
97.—Dumbarton Oaks Research Library and Collections, Washington, D.C.
98.—Cabinet d'Estampes, Bibliothèque Nationale, Paris.
99.—Musée Château, Versailles, Lauros-Giraudon, Photographie Giraudon, Paris.
100.—Salon des Sources, Versailles, Lauros-Giraudon, Photographie Giraudon, Paris.
101.—Louvre, Cabinet des Dessins, Documentation Photographique de la Réunion des Musées Nationaux, Paris.
102.—Dumbarton Oaks Research Library and Collections, Washington, D.C.
103.—Cabinet d'Estampes, Bibliothèque Nationale, Paris.
104.—Louvre, Cabinet des Dessins, Documentation Photographique de la Réunion des Musées Nationaux, Paris.
105.—Louvre, Cabinet des Dessins, Documentation Photographique de la Réunion des Musées Nationaux, Paris.
106.—Cabinet d'Estampes, Bibliothèque Nationale, Paris.
107.—Louvre, Cabinet des Dessins, Documentation Photographique de la Réunion des Musées Nationaux, Paris.

108.—Cabinet d'Estampes, Bibliothèque Nationale, Paris.
109.—Louvre, Cabinet des Dessins, Documentation Photographique de la Réunion des Musées Nationaux, Paris.
110.—Dumbarton Oaks Research Library and Research Collection, Washington, D.C.
111.—Cabinet d'Estampes, Bibliothèque Nationale, Paris.
112.—Louvre, Cabinet des Dessins, Documentation Photographique de la Réunion des Musées Nationaux, Paris.
113.—H. Roger-Viollet, Paris.
114.—Louvre, Cabinet des Dessins, Documentation Photographique de la Réunion des Musées Nationaux, Paris.
115.—Louvre, Cabinet des Dessins, Documentation Photographique de la Réunion des Musées Nationaux, Paris.
116.—Musée Île de France, Photographie Giraudon, Paris.
117.—Cabinet d'Estampes, Bibliothèque Nationale, Paris.
118.—Collection of author.
119.—Service Photographique des Archives Nationales, Paris.
120.—Service Photographique des Archives Nationales, Paris.
121.—Musée Carnavalet, Paris.
122.—Courtesy Museum of Fine Arts, Boston.
123.—Louvre, Cabinet des Dessins, Documentation Photographique de la Réunion des Musées Nationaux, Paris.
124.—Collection of author.
125.—Louvre, Photographie Giraudon, Paris.
126.—Musée des Beaux-Arts, Orléans.
127.—Musée Île de France, Photographie Giraudon, Paris.
128.—Dumbarton Oaks Research Library and Collections, Washington, D.C.
129.—Dumbarton Oaks Research Library and Collections, Washington, D.C.
130.—Caisse Nationale des Monuments Historiques et des Sites, ATGET/c. Arch. Phot. Paris/S.P.A.D.E.M.
131.—Photograph Courtesy Patrick Bracco
132.—Collection of author.
133.—Archives Nationales, Paris.
134.—Dumbarton Oaks Research Library and Collections, Washington, D.C.
135.—Dumbarton Oaks Research Library and Collections, Washington, D.C.
136.—Dumbarton Oaks Research Library and Collections, Washington, D.C.
137.—Collection of author.
138.—Cabinet d'Estampes, Bibliothèque Nationale, Paris.
139.—Caisse Nationale des Monuments Historiques et des Sites, Arch. Phot. Paris.
140.—Dumbarton Oaks Research Library and Collections, Washington, D.C.
141.—Dumbarton Oaks Research Library and Collections, Washington, D.C.
142.—Cabinet d'Estampes, Bibliothèque Nationale, Paris.
143.—Dumbarton Oaks Research Library and Collections, Washington, D.C.
144.—Photograph Courtesy Patrick Bracco.
145.—Dumbarton Oaks Research Library and Collections, Washington, D.C.
146.—Dumbarton Oaks Research Library and Collections, Washington, D.C.
147.—Cabinet d'Estampes, Bibliothèque Nationale, Paris.
148.—Cabinet d'Estampes, Bibliothèque Nationale, Paris.
149.—Cabinet d'Estampes, Bibliothèque Nationale, Paris.
150.—Caisse Nationale des Monuments Historiques et des Sites, Arch. Phot. Paris. (Bibliothèque Historique de la Ville de Paris.)
151.—Cabinet d'Estampes, Bibliothèque Nationale, Paris.
152.—Caisse Nationale des Monuments Historiques et des Sites, Arch. Phot. Paris.
153.—Collection of author.
154.—Collection of author.
155.—Collection of author.
156.—Photograph by author.
157.—Collection of author.
158.—H. Roger Viollet, Collection Viollet, Paris.
159.—Collection of author.
160.—H. Roger Viollet, Paris.
161.—Photographie Giraudon, Paris.
162.—Collection of author.
163.—Cabinet d'Estampes, Bibliothèque Nationale, Paris.
164.—Photograph courtesy Patrick Bracco.
165.—Seattle Art Museum, Seattle, Washington.
166.—Dumbarton Oaks Research Library and Collections, Washington, D.C.
167.—Collection of author.
168.—Collection of author.